Jackson Jones
The Tale of a Boy, an Elf, and a Very Stinky Fish

Jackson Jones
The Tale of a Boy, an Elf, and a Very Stinky Fish

written by
Jenn Kelly

illustrated by
Ariane Elsammak

ZONDERVAN.com/
AUTHORTRACKER
follow your favorite authors

ZONDERKIDZ

Jackson Jones: The Tale of a Boy, an Elf, and a Very Stinky Fish
Copyright © 2010 Jennifer Kelly
Illustrations © 2010 Ariane Elsammak

This title is also available as a Zondervan ebook.
Visit www.zondervan.com/ebooks.

Requests for information should be addressed to:
Zonderkidz, Grand Rapids, Michigan 49530

Library of Congress Cataloging-in-Publication Data

Kelly, Jennifer, 1973-
    Jackson Jones : the tale of a boy, an elf, and a very stinky fish / by Jennifer Kelly ;
illustrations by Ariane Elsammak.
       p.   cm.
    Summary: When ten-year-old Jackson falls into Great Aunt Harriet's very big
hair, he finds a wealth of amazing things including a new friend, Meeka the elf,
perilous dangers that allow him to be a hero, and even his own story.
    ISBN 978-0-310-72079-9 (hardcover)
    [1. Adventure and adventurers—Fiction. 2. Heroes—Fiction. 3. Authorship—
Fiction. 4. Elves—Fiction. 5. Hair—Fiction. 6. Humorous stories.] I. Elsammak,
Ariane, ill. II. Title.
PZ7.K29622Jac   2010
[Fic]—dc22   2010013101

Editor: Kathleen Kerr
Art direction: Sarah Molegraaf
Cover design: Ariane Elsammak
Interior design: Carlos Estrada and Sherri L. Hoffman

Printed in the United States of America

10 11 12 13 14 15 /DCI/ 22 21 20 19 18 17 16 15 14 13 12 11 10 9 8 7 6 5 4 3 2 1

For my three boys:
God, Danny, and Jackson
I adore you.

chapter

Table of Contents

The First Chapter

Jackson didn't know it yet, but in a faraway place, closer than he could imagine, a little creature was sighing in frustration.

This little creature was sighing because she had absolutely no idea what to do. This wasn't a surprise in itself, especially if you knew her. She *never* had any idea what to do.

The trap door was shut.

Locked, in fact.

It wasn't *supposed* to be locked.

It was *supposed* to be *un*locked.

And wide open.

She was supposed to unlock it and open it, so that it would no longer be locked and unopened.

But given that Meeka was just that kind of elf, she had forgotten the key.

So there she stood, at the top of a thirty-foot ladder, trying to unlock a trap door with a dead, smelly fish.

No Longer the First Chapter

Jackson rolled over and opened his eyes. He looked at the clock. Still early. His eyes closed. He began to dream again, but then something tickled his mind. What was so important about today?

Oh yes.

Family reunion day.

A Chapter that Has a Secret in It

Jackson had a lot of family members.

That didn't mean his dad had four arms or his aunt had twelve legs, but what it did mean was there were a lot of people in his family.

He had a mom, a dad, one brother, one sister, seven aunts, eight uncles, and twenty-four cousins. They were a close family. Jackson saw his family *all* the time. What with birthdays, anniversaries, soccer games, talent shows, science fairs, and vacations, life was ... insane. And Christmas was just an imbroglio, as you can imagine. (*Imbroglio* is like when you're playing tag with twenty other kids ... in the kitchen ... and your mom is cooking ... and the dog just threw up.)

However (and this is a rather large however, meaning you are about to read something that is a big deal, so pay attention), HOWEVER, Jackson had just moved. Not just him, but his entire family. Not all of his aunts and uncles and cousins and all of their imbroglios, but just Jackson and his mom, dad, brother, and sister. Not only did they just move, but they moved far, far away. This meant no more imbroglios for a while.

Of course Jackson should have been mad. But as hard as he tried to be mad, he couldn't be. You see, Jackson's mom was a writer. And not just any writer,

but a really good one. Not only was she a really good writer, she was also a kind-hearted writer. This meant she didn't turn into one of those writers who demand first-class treatment everywhere they go, like demanding steak and chocolate ice cream on a plane when they are only serving peanuts. But because Jackson's mom was such a good writer, she had to do research in a place that was far away. But the reason Jackson couldn't be mad was because he understood. He understood how important writing was to his mom ... because writing was important to him.

You see, Jackson had a secret. A secret only he and his mom knew about.

Jackson wanted to be a writer too.

Every Sunday night, after church was finished and the huge lunch was finished and they had all gone for a healthy walk, admiring trees and ponds and silly little ducks, after everyone had gone into their own rooms to just "take it down a notch," Jackson would go into his mother's studio, sit in the huge leather chair, and drink hot chocolate while she read his stories and talked to him as a writer, but with the kind heart of a mom. Sometimes they would talk about important things, like what he would write about next, about the clouds they had seen that day, and about how fast he was growing. Maybe growing fast isn't important to a ten-and-a-half-year old, but it's always important to a mom. And sometimes they would talk about unimportant things, such as ... well, actually, there's no such thing as unimportant things to talk about.

But I suppose you're wondering more about Jackson.

Jackson was an average-looking ten-and-a-half-year-old boy. He was a little on the small side. He had blondish-brown hair and his eyes were a bluish-grayish-greenish brown. He did have very straight teeth, however, which meant he had a very nice smile.

Jackson was in sixth grade. Yes, he should have been in fifth grade, but after a ten-minute coffee break (which included an unpleasant piece of fruitcake), the principal decided Jackson would be in sixth grade. They had more desks, you see. That was a ridiculous decision of course, but one makes ridiculous decisions when eating unpleasant cake. Wars have been known to break out over leaders eating dry sponge cake, and there is speculation that King Henry VIII had his fifth wife disposed of because she served him plain white cake instead of the raspberry he craved.

So Jackson didn't really fit in at his new school. All of the other kids had known each other for a long time and Jackson was the new kid. And he was the smallest. He got picked last for games at recess. He made the baseball team only because they were short a player. And when he did play, I'm sorry to tell you, he was terrible. And he knew he was terrible.

Jackson loved to read. It passed the time at recess when he didn't feel like being picked last that day. He

also loved writing stories. Oh, the stories he'd written! Jackson was always the hero, of course.

The unassuming hero who stepped in at the last minute to save the universe.

The unassuming hero who saved the entire village from a raging fire.

The unassuming hero who saved the cat up the tree, received a medal from the mayor, and got a thank-you parade that included those old guys who drove around in little cars.

The unassuming hero who could figure out algebra.

A Chapter that Involves an Awful Mishap with a Kangaroo

Jackson! Time to get up!" his mother yelled from the downstairs kitchen.

Jackson slid out of bed. As he put on his jeans and a clean-ish shirt, he thought about what the day would entail.

Family reunion day meant that Jackson's whole entire family (aunts, uncles, cousins, and all of their arms and legs) were coming over for a big party. He hadn't seen them all in months! They would eat barbecued tofu dogs and bean burgers (his Aunt Gertrude had become a vegetarian after an awful mishap with a kangaroo, but we won't get into that right now), fresh-cut veggies (obviously), baked potato chips (you got used to them), and baked beet risotto (don't even ask).

They would play Hide-and-Seek and Capture the Flag and swim in the creek. At night they would sit around the bonfire, roasting tofu marshmallows and catch fireflies in their hands. They would squish their little glowing bodies between their fingers and smear the goop on their teeth and have glow-in-the-dark smiles.

Good times.

When Jackson came down to the kitchen his mom already had her anxious face on. Her hair was a big frizz ball, getting frizzier by the second as she stirred the beet risotto over the hot stove. His sister poured the baked potato chips into party bowls. A mound of vegetables waited on the counter to be cut up. Jackson's sister looked up and stuck her tongue out at him. He scowled at her. What else can you do to a six-year-old? Actually, don't answer that.

"Mom! Jackson's making that face again!" she whined.

Jackson's mom didn't even turn around. "Jackson, quit picking on your sister."

"But Mom, I'm not! She's the one ..." he protested.

"Look, it's a really big day for everyone, okay? And we are definitely behind schedule. Just go upstairs and get your room ready for your aunt. You can cut the vegetables when you're done."

Jackson ran out of the kitchen and up the stairs. But his steps faltered. He had forgotten.

Great-Aunt Harriett would be
... staying
   ... in
     ... Jackson's
       ... room.

chapter 5

A Very Hairy Chapter

Great-Aunt Harriett always made Jackson a *little* uncomfortable. It wasn't because she wore funny dresses. It wasn't because she smelled like mothballs. And it wasn't even because she was "Oh-So-Very Old." And she was "Oh-So-Very Old." Jackson figured she was a hundred and twelve years old. Now that's old. Especially if you're a dog. Why, that's seven hundred eighty-four years old!

No, it wasn't the funny dresses, the mothballs, or being seven hundred eighty-four years old.

It was her hair.

Yes, you read that correctly: her hair.

Jackson was uncomfortable because of her hair.

I'm sure you must think he was overreacting. How could anyone be afraid of hair? But you don't understand. She had very, very, very, very, very, very, very big hair.

Oh, I know you've seen some big hair before. At proms and debutante balls, most cheerleaders, in '80s music videos, in southern Texas, and on the woman who sits right in front of you at the movie theater. But her hair was even bigger.

Imagine, if you will, a very large wedding cake. You know the kind they serve at all the best weddings? Not at the boring weddings where you eat dry chicken and listen to hours of speeches about how the bride cut her first tooth. And the wedding cake is flavorless enough to invoke a full-blown political revolt.

I'm talking about the awesome weddings where your parents let you run around without your suit jacket on. Where you have the option of dancing the Hokey Pokey or touring the buffet again. And where the wedding cake is big enough for everyone to get a blue sugary rose to stain their teeth.

Great-Aunt Harriet's hair was even bigger than that. It was a strange grayish-red color and it was oh-so-very thick. So thick, in fact, that when the wind blew, it stood completely still. Once, during a tornado, she hid a little dog in there and afterward they had tea.

Great-Aunt Harriett was also very, very, very, very, very, very, very short.

So short, in fact, that if you stood up straight you would talk to hair. If you bent over at the waist you would talk to hair. If you sat on the ground you could see her scrunched-up little face, crinkled-apple cheeks, squinty eyes behind her very thick glasses, and her toothless mouth.

If Jackson didn't sit on the floor to talk to her, she would talk directly to his belly button. It is never a pleasant sensation having someone talk to your belly button. Unless, of course, they *want* to talk to your belly button. But we won't get into that right now.

Great-Aunt Harriett *loved* to talk. She would chatter on and on about old houses, birds, and keys. (Not piano keys, but keys that open doors.) She didn't have any teeth in her tiny, puckered mouth, so she mumbled and lisped a lot. And when she mumbled and lisped, bits of spit sprayed all over everything. This usually made for messy (and wet) conversations. And she would go on and on, sometimes asking a question, but since she was very, very, very hard of hearing (maybe it was all that hair?), she never really heard the answers. For example:

Great-Aunt Harriett: "So how are you doing in school, Jackson?" (Actually, it sounded like "Tho how aw you doin thcoo, Jackthon?" but I've translated for you.)

Jackson: "It's summertime, Great-Aunt Harriett. I'm not in school right now."

Great-Aunt Harriett: "You're captain of the tuba-bassoon group?"

Jackson: "No, I said I'm not in school right now. I don't even like the tuba! Or the bassoon! I don't even play an instrument!"

Great-Aunt Harriett: "You know, that reminds me of the birds I saw last night. They were so lovely. They just kept singing the most beautiful songs. Maybe you can play those songs on your bassoon for me?"

And so on.

One thing Great-Aunt Harriett always said was, "Find your story!"

But there was a slight problem. It was lovely that she told him to find his own story, because that was a very nice thing to say, and it was very encouraging, especially for people who were, at that moment, living their stories or perhaps on the verge of making the decision to do just that.

The slight problem was that:

Jackson ...

    did ...

        not ...

            have ...

                a ...

                    story.

He was only ten and a half, for goodness' sakes! How on earth could he tell his story if he didn't know what it was? I mean, sure, he'd like to play baseball a little better. Who wouldn't? And of course it would be pretty neat to see his stories published, but all writers want that. It would also be nice to have a few friends ... but that's not really a story.

Is it?

chapter

6

In Which We Learn about Diplomacy

It's never fun to share your room with relatives, especially when you have a smallish bed in your smallish room. You end up on the floor, possibly even *under* your bed. And the food wrappers that you forgot to throw out are crackling under your sleeping bag, and something seems to be growing on that banana peel. What's worse is when you sleep with your cousin on the sofa bed in the basement, and he's twitching and snoring and drooling on *your* pillow the whole night. No, that's not much fun at all. Relatives should just stay in a hotel, but asking them to do so is just not hospitable. So they'll stay in your room, and you'll just learn to like it.

Jackson tried arguing, diplomatically of course, about Great-Aunt Harriett staying in his room. Diplomatic is like when you tell your big sister to stay out of your room or you'll tell mom what she wrote in her diary. (Not that I condone diary reading. That's an invasion of privacy.)

Jackson's mom pulled him into her studio and sat him down. She diplomatically told him that Great-Aunt Harriett had had a very hard life, that she was very old, and could they cut her some slack? Diplomatically

means, "Chill out little guy. I love you, but I'm the boss, and you will be gracious about sharing your room."

It was a good thing that Jackson had an awesome bunk bed. He *loved* his bunk bed. He had a fort made out of old green sheets on the top bunk. He kept a flashlight up there and, underneath his signed picture of Reggie Jackson, a pen and a notebook.

Jackson would sleep on the top and Great-Aunt Harriett would be on the bottom bunk.

chapter

7

In Which This Book Begins

And now the adventure begins.

chapter

8

In Which This Book
Really Begins

It had been a perfect family reunion day. A day full of tofu dogs and bean burgers, baked potato chips, hiding the beet risotto in a bun (because the dog sure wouldn't eat it), hide-and-seek, capture the flag, firefly goop, and swimming in the creek. Jackson's dad even caught a horsefly with his bare hands (his bare hands!) and tied a piece of long hair around the horsefly's belly so that when it tried to fly away, he could yank it back. Jackson beamed with pride. His dad was so cool.

Jackson had a perfect day, but he was looking forward to bed. He could use some downtime.

He meticulously brushed and flossed his teeth, then practiced his friendly smile in the mirror.

"Hi, I'm Jackson," he smiled into the mirror. Jackson frowned and tried again.

"Do you want to play with me today?"

He wet his hair and brushed it up into a Mohawk. Not bad.

"Dude, did you, like see the game, like, last night?" The mirror didn't reply.

"Hey, have you ever read ..."

But cool guys don't read books. Jackson sighed. *Why couldn't there be just one other dork at school?*

Why couldn't there be just one person who didn't have a friend yet?

But Jackson knew. He knew how it was to be the new kid in school. He knew it would take a while for everyone to like him. And then they would *really* like him. Jackson quickly blinked back hot tears. They would see that he was a cool guy too. But no crying. Not tonight. He frowned and patted the tips of his Mohawk. *No more reading at school. I'll be the cool guy everyone wants to hang out with.*

Jackson climbed into his favorite red pajamas and stretched out on the top bunk. He snuggled down into his cozy sheets. He paused in reaching for his book.

But I can read at home, he reminded himself.

A huffing and a puffing made Jackson look up from his book. Great-Aunt Harriett trundled in, dragging herself over to the bottom bunk. She plunked herself down heavily, shaking the whole bunk bed. She let out a big sigh and smacked her toothless gums. Jackson slid further under his blankets and turned the page very quietly.

Oh dear, she's started to talk.

"Jackson dear, have I ever told you about the house I grew up in?"

"Yes, Great-Aunt Harriett. Many times." (*page turn*)

"Well, let me tell you about my house. It was a beautiful house, dear." (She obviously hadn't heard him.)

"It had a big front porch ..."

"It had a big front porch that my daddy built way back when I was just a little girl. And if you followed that porch all the way around to the back of the house, there were steps that led into ..."

"... the garden that you played in." (*page turn*)

"... the garden that I played in. It was a lovely garden. And behind the garden was a little shed that my daddy built for the gardener to keep his tools in. Oh, what was his name?"

"Mr. Shaw." Jackson sighed quietly.

"Mr. Shaw. Oh my, he was a nice man. He taught me all kinds of things about flowers and birds. He even let me have a key to the shed so I could hide in it and pretend it was my own little house. He knew so much about birds. He knew so much about ..."

Great-Aunt Harriett's eyes shut. The little wrinkles were less pronounced as her eyes closed. Jackson held his breath, waiting.

"Birds ... houses ... gold key," she murmured. All was quiet. Jackson let his breath out.

"Find your story!" she sighed. And then she began to snore.

Jackson had wondered earlier if maybe Great-Aunt Harriett would die in his bottom bunk bed, which was a reasonable thought because she was Oh-So-Very Old. But Dad said that as long as she was snoring, she was fine.

Jackson could NOT fall asleep.

At all.

He tossed one way, his legs tangling in the dark blue sheets.

He tossed the other, his legs tangling again.

He even learned how to toss a new way, which I can't reveal to you because it's something you will have to figure out for yourself some night when you can't sleep.

Jackson sighed, staring at the ceiling. He sighed again, staring at the inside of his eyelids. *Would the flashlight wake her up?* Jackson turned over quietly and poked his head over the edge to look at Great-Aunt Harriett below.

Her body twitched as she snored. That was a good sign. Her creepy toothless mouth opened and closed with each rasp. She hacked and coughed violently and then resumed snoring.

Jackson could not take his eyes away. It was so gross, and yet so fascinating. Her little eyelids were covered in deep wrinkles. Her dried-out apple cheeks puffed up and sank with each breath. Jackson looked at her hair.

The moonlight that snuck in the window made her hair glow. Jackson was mesmerized by it. He became sleepy as he stared at it. The shimmering glow, so hypnotic, so sleepy ... Jackson's eyes had almost shut.

Her hair twitched.

chapter 9

In Which There Will Be
Absolutely No Crying

"Oh, for CRYING OUT LOUD!" A large, juicy fish hit the floor. A pike, in fact.

The little creature sat on one of the ladder's rungs and sighed, pushing her long, wispy brown hair out of her face. She hadn't even noticed the bits of stinky fish gunk in her hair.

Of course a fish wouldn't open a locked door. Why would she even think that? And what was she going to do?

The fish idea had been hers, of course. When she arrived at the locked trapdoor late and without the key, she had been so surprised, so embarrassed, so mortified that she was desperate for ideas. She had dug through her workbag, searching for anything that would help. The barrette hadn't worked. It was as useless at picking a lock as it was at keeping her crazy hair out of her face. The key she had origami-ed out of paper kept bending and then finally tore. Her pen nib had broken, staining her right hand and most of her work shirt a fabulous pink. The fish had been her last choice. She pried open his dead mouth, trying to use his teeth, but as we all know, fish are rather slippery and uncooperative, especially when they are dead. So now it lay at the bottom of the ladder.

Meeka's fist smacked the door. Tiny, frustrated tears threatened to fall. She would *not* cry. She *would not* cry. *She would not cry!* How on earth could she be taken seriously if she cried every time she messed up? Meeka sighed and climbed back down the ladder. Time to face the inevitable.

In Which Nothing Makes Sense

If your parents made you put down this book after the last chapter, I'm very sorry. Some parents have rules like that, only letting their children read a few chapters before bedtime. However, to console you, when you are an adult you can stay up as late as you want and read as much as you want.

Wait, what?

Jackson pinched himself. Her hair twitched again. Jackson was ... well, you tell me. I mean, how would you feel if you saw her hair twitch?

Jackson slowly leaned over the edge. *What if I touch it? What if something comes out?*

Jackson leaned
just a little bit far-
ther over the edge.
His toes dug into
the crack between
his mattress and
the wall. Was it his
imagination or did he
smell roast beef? And
leather? And ... what
was that? Dead fish?
And ...

... he fell.

Jackson couldn't breathe.

"Oh n ...!"

That was all that came out of Jackson's mouth before he ate a mouthful of hair. He coughed and grabbed as his hands dug frantically at the hair in his mouth. His left hand grasped the air and touched something solid. He stepped close to the wall, pushing the hair out of his face with his arms. A sign hung on the wall of hair.

Welcome
to
Great-Aunt Harriet's Hair

Hours of operation are
8 a.m.–5 p.m. daily.
Author's Tours begin every hour on the hour.
We close every 7th and 18th day
for reconstruction and cleanup.

If you need assistance, please ring the bell.
For your own safety and protection,
please wear the protective glasses.
We are not liable for hair getting into eyes,
bad hair days, or hair strangling.
Have a nice day.

Jackson frowned. *It's definitely past five o'clock.* Underneath was the fine print.

Jackson stepped closer, pushing the hair out of his eyes and squinted.

"If you need assistance, please ring the bell.
For your own safety,
please wear the protective glasses.
We are not liable for hair getting into eyes,
bad hair days, or hair strangling.
Have a nice day."

Jackson searched the walls blindly and found a pair of goggles hanging on a hook. He put them on. He could see! All the tendrils of hair turned into tunnels and hallways, like a maze. He was looking around for a bell when a sweet voice chirped beside him.

chapter 11

In Which We Meet Meeka and Her Dead, Smelly Fish

If you're taking turns reading with your mom, dad, or teacher, at least you got to read a small chapter so it wasn't too hard. If your mom, dad, or teacher read the last chapter, then I apologize in advance, as this chapter might be long. So take a sip of water and read on.

"May I help you, sir?" squeaked the little ... thing. What was it? An elf? And why was she holding a dead, smelly fish?

"Um, well, uh, I'm ... uh ... I'm Jackson."

The creature in front of him was different-looking, no doubt about it. She was tiny, only coming up to his shoulder. Her long brown hair was tied back, but she had stray pieces everywhere, even in her mouth. She wore a brown uniform of some sort, with a fabulous pink splotch on the front of it. But it wasn't buttoned properly, and the hem of her skirt hung slightly askew. Her red neckerchief was a messy bow,

41

and the worn leather pouch around her waist bulged with indistinguishable items. (*Indistinguishable* is like when you sneak under the Christmas tree and for the life of you can't figure out what's inside those wrapped presents.) Her big, long-lashed brown eyes fixed on Jackson as she smiled a big smile at him.

"Are you here for the Author's Tours, sir? We are closed you know, the hours of operation being eight a.m. to five p.m., and we are closed every seventh and eighteeth day for reconstruction and clean up. And a tour guide is required you see," she chirped.

"I didn't even know there was a tour," said Jackson. "I mean, I just fell into Great-Aunt Harriett's hair and I ended up here. Which authors do you mean? Is Jules Verne in here? Where is 'here,' anyway?" He craned his neck to look down the hallways, which of course is a very ineffective way to look down hallways.

"Why, you're in Great-Aunt Harriett's hair!" The elf gestured grandly down the hallway.

Jackson looked at her, noticing her name tag. "Your name is Meeka?"

Her jaw dropped open in bewilderment. Bewilderment is like when you look outside and it's snowing. And it's July.

"How do you know my name? Are you an elf?" Her eyes narrowed suspiciously. "Do you work here?" She quickly hid the dead fish behind her back.

"What? No! I'm not an elf! I'm a boy! And I can read, you know."

"I see! Well, in that case, I *am* an elf. Well, not yet. You can't become a full-fledged elf until you get out of touring, but we won't get into that right now."

"So, wanna go on a tour? We don't normally do tours after five o'clock, but seeing as how I'm up and about anyway ..." Her voice trailed off as she looked down at the fish in her hands. Her face turned bright strawberry red and she jammed the smelly, dead fish into her workbag. She cleared her throat.

"There are many rooms to visit. Is there a specific room you would like to see first?" Meeka asked, wiping her hands on her skirt.

"How many rooms are in here, exactly?"

Meeka's big brown eyes looked up at the ceiling as she ticked off her fingers, counting quietly. "Um, eleven-twenty."

"Eleven-twenty isn't a number."

Meeka turned her eyes on Jackson. "Eleven-twenty is too a number. It comes before the twelve-somethings," she argued.

Jackson back-pedaled. "My mistake."

"Quite all right!" Meeka laughed. "This is a very big place."

Jackson thought about the size of Great-Aunt Harriett's hair and agreed. It was a lot of hair. I mean, a *lot* of hair.

"Why don't you just take me wherever you want?" Jackson said.

Meeka's eyes grew even bigger. "Are you sure?"

Jackson shrugged his shoulders, "Why not?"

Meeka's smile disappeared as she became very serious. She straightened the hem of her skirt and flattened her stray hairs. She sniffed importantly and marched to one of the cabinets hanging on the wall.

"You'll need this," she announced. She handed him a beautiful leather satchel. It had a thick leather strap with engravings of winding vines. The bag itself smelled of warm leather and was soft to the touch. Jackson slung it over his head and shoulder. It sat perfectly in the crook of his neck. His fingers found the heavy brass clasp, and he opened it. Inside was a pen, a flashlight, and running shoes.

Jackson's eyebrows shot up. "You're giving me this?"

Meeka nodded sagely. (*Sagely* means you are trying your hardest to look smart without laughing. This is not an easy task.) "We like everyone to be prepared."

Jackson pulled the shoes out and slipped them on. They fit him perfectly.

"How did you know my size?" he asked.

Meeka shrugged. "I wouldn't be a very good tour guide if I wasn't prepared." She turned.

"We go this way."

In Which the Tour Begins

Jackson looked around him as he followed Meeka down the hall. The grayish-red walls curved up into an arched ceiling overhead. They didn't look like they were made of hair, but as you stepped closer you could see all of the hairs intertwined into an elaborate braid.

"Why is it called the Author's tour? Are we going to meet any authors?" Jackson asked excitedly. He hoped so. *He* loved meeting authors.

Meeka shuffled her shoulders. "Um ... that's not quite what it means."

"Oh, you mean there's a Shakespeare wing or a Lewis Carroll tearoom. That kind of thing?"

"Not exactly." Meeka began to walk faster.

"Well what kind of thing is it?"

"Um, it's kind of hard to explain ..." She trailed off. "Well, the first room we're going to see is fantastic! It's the

room that I think everyone should visit first. The Book Room."

"I already have a lot of books you know. I have *Jaws* and *20,000 Leagues Under the Sea*, and my mom reads me *Alice in Wonderland* at bedtime ..." Jackson stopped, embarrassed. He loved to snuggle in with his mom and a hot chocolate, listening to her voice rise and fall as she read his favorite books. But no one needed to know that, especially a little elf he barely knew.

"But I bet you've never seen the books inside Great-Aunt Harriett's hair!" Meeka argued.

Jackson had to nod his head in agreement. That was true.

"Here we are!" she announced. And there they were indeed. A big, brown door was nestled into the wall with a big black sign on it.

"Stand back please, sir," said Meeka, and she knocked. The big, brown door swung heavily into the room, and faint smells of wood polish tickled Jackson's nose.

"Our first room," Meeka declared.

They walked in.

chapter

13

In Which We Enter
the Book Room

You have probably been inside a bookstore before. You might have even been inside an *old* bookstore, or at least been dragged into one. But have you ever been in an old, well-kept bookstore? You know, the kind with wood floors that are so lustrous you can see your reflection in them? Off to the side is a wrought-iron staircase that spirals up to the second floor, where more books are waiting for you to investigate. Tall bookshelves that go from floor to ceiling are crammed with old books written by many, many authors. The books arc in excellent condition of course, and they are all hardcover, some even with hand-painted drawings. A tall, wooden ladder slides along these bookshelves so your fingers can trail the spines as you look for that special book. At the far end is a wall made up of stained-glass windows that cast shifting colors onto the polished floor. The stone fireplace in the corner is lit with a cheery blaze to keep you company as you sit reading in the big, green, overstuffed chair. You drink hot chocolate with extra whipped cream and chocolate sprinkles that you are careful not to spill because you wouldn't dare spill anything in a place like this. And as you sip and read, you hear lovely classical music that even you, a classical-music hater, enjoy.

The Book Room was exactly such a room.

Jackson felt the serenity within the room. (*Serenity* is like when it's 7:00 on a Saturday morning and the house is quiet and you're watching cartoons while eating two full bowls of sugar flakes.) He walked slowly around, admiring the books, the bookshelves, and the tall, wooden ladder. He smiled at the wrought-iron staircase that spiraled up to the second floor. Meeka threw her tour guide's pouch onto the big, green, over-stuffed chair and then lay down on the floor. She stuck her tongue out, making faces at her reflection in the shiny wood.

Jackson noticed a counter in the corner.

The counter was made of polished, dark wood and curved slightly around to a deep maroon velvet-

curtained doorway. On the well-polished counter sat a well-polished silver bell. And beside the well-polished silver bell was a little white card with gold script.

The gold script read:

Ting the bell for service.

Jackson touched his index finger to the well-polished bell and tapped down on the button. A clear sound reverberated off the walls and into his skin. As the "ting" faded, a very tall man slipped out from behind the deep maroon velvet curtain in the doorway.

chapter

14

The Chapter after That

He was old. White tufts of hair created little fluffy clouds around his ears. His dark blue eyes were serious, but there was a joke twinkling behind them. You know the kind of eyes that read serious newspaper articles but laugh at the cartoons as well? He wore a well-worn, bright green blazer with a sky-blue dress shirt underneath. His tie was deep red with little black question marks all over it. His pants matched the blazer, and his shoes, I'm happy to say, were bright red high-cut sneakers. (My favorite suits are the ones you can wear with bright red sneakers.) He stood up very straight as though he had proper posture training. A small smile danced behind his frown.

"May I help you, sir?" the gentleman asked. His voice was very serious, very dignified, and very polite.

Jackson was at a loss for words. He was in awe.

You know when you go to meet the Queen and you are really excited? So you put on your best clothes and wet down your cowlick, but when you get there you have absolutely no idea what to say to her? So when you open your mouth, you say something ridiculous like, "Shame about the weather, your Highness," or "Are your roses doing well, your Highness?" And if you really want to humiliate yourself, you say, "Don't all those cucumber sandwiches make you gassy?" Well, that's

exactly how Jackson felt. This gentleman was eccentric and classy—gracious even. Almost like a kindly grandfather, but one who was a butler as well. I know it's a strange contrast, but someday when you meet him, you will completely understand.

"I don't know. I'm n-not really s-sure what I'm looking for, or if I'm looking for anything. I'm on a t-tour, you see." Jackson smoothed his wrinkly red pajamas, wishing he had put on some jeans. He swallowed. "Are you an author?"

The gentleman looked over at Meeka. She lay on her stomach, her face an inch from the floor. She was humming and her tongue was sticking out. The gentleman's white, bushy right eyebrow arched in a most dignified way, and he looked back at Jackson. "Perhaps sir would care to look around in our **Ask** section," he said in a very serious, very dignified, and very polite voice.

"What do you mean?"

The gentleman turned to the left, gracefully extending his long arm, and pointed the direction to go. He used his whole hand to point and not just a finger, as using one finger is impolite, of course.

"If you need anything else, sir, please do not hesitate to ask. I am Sir Shaw." And he silently slipped behind the dark maroon velvet curtain.

Jackson looked over at Meeka, who had her fingers in her ears and was rolling her eyes about. She giggled quietly to herself.

Jackson approached a wooden archway that led into another room. A large sign hung over the entrance. It was black, with large white writing that read:

"Ask what?" Jackson muttered, and he entered the room.

chapter

15

In Which There Are Too Many Books (As if That's Possible)

The room was small and consisted of only one bookshelf. Jackson approached the bookshelf, scanning the books on display. Their covers were blank. He picked one up and opened it. Empty. He picked up another. Nothing inside at all.

"How is this supposed to help?"

Letters began to dance on the covers, forming titles.

How to Decipher Riddles,

How to Stop Your Tour Guide from Making Faces on the Floor,

How to Choose a Book, and

*How to Ask the Right Questions in the **Ask** Section of the Book Room.*

Jackson picked up the last one. Its creamy yellow pages were bound in dark leather. He opened to the first page and read aloud:

"Ask for what you want help with."

Jackson put the book back. *What I want?* His eyebrows frowned in concentration. "Well, what do I want?" he wondered aloud.

A magical tinkling filled the air. The same kind of wonderful magical tinkling that tells you that something wonderful is about to happen. The books changed. The covers morphed into different colors, their titles changing into new titles. Jackson scratched his head in wonderment.

How to Win Baseball Games,

How to Write Amazing Stories, and

How to Win Arguments with Your Parents.

Ooh, that had to be a good one. His fingers reached up, but stopped as a title appeared on a purple book.

How to Hide Your Beet Risotto 17 Different Ways.

An orange one read, *How to be Cool in School.*

How to Influence Friends and Win People, read a raspberry-colored book.

Perfect.

Jackson picked it up and began to walk toward the well-polished counter.

Uh-oh.

Jackson shrugged off his satchel and checked inside. He groaned. Of course there was no money in it. Jackson looked around. The title changed on a green book in front of him.

How to Steal Without Getting Caught.

Jackson was tempted.

Very tempted.

The title morphed again: *How to Give into Temptation Without Feeling Guilty.*

Jackson chose not to look. He had a conscience after all. He was putting the book back when something caught his eye. Up on the shelf was a plain, ordinary-looking brown book. He picked it up.

How to Be Yourself.

Jackson paused, holding his breath. *I want people to like me. I want to have friends. I want to be one of the cool guys who makes everyone laugh, who people want to hang out with. But maybe I don't have to be cool for people to like me. What do I do?*

Another book title changed in front of him.

How to Make a Decision.

Jackson was getting a headache. This was some pretty serious stress.

"We need to continue with the tour," Meeka squeaked, appearing at his elbow. Her hair was a mess with a big squirrel's nest in the back. (Not an actual squirrel's nest. It was just a messy knot, although you never know.) Meeka looked at the book in Jackson's hands.

"Oh, no, you MUST get *How to Be Cool in School!* Then you would have oh-so-many friends! I would LO-OOVE to have many friends. Even just one friend would be wonderful," she added wistfully, looking up at Jackson from beneath her long eyelashes.

"I'll be your friend."

"Really? I have my very own friend?" And she threw her little arms around him, hugging him with surprising force. "Then you don't need that book because I'm your friend too!" She skipped out of the room and tossed herself on to the big, green, overstuffed chair by the fireplace. She picked up a hot chocolate with extra whipped cream and chocolate sprinkles and slurped

it loudly. The extra whipped cream made interestingly gross noises as she inhaled it.

"No, I guess I don't need it," Jackson whispered to himself. He studied the ordinary-looking brown book in his other hand. It felt cool and heavy. He turned it one way and then the other. It felt like a very important book.

"Have you found what you are looking for, sir?" asked a very serious voice that was also very dignified and very polite.

Jackson gave Sir Shaw an unintentionally guilty look.

"I think I have, but ..." Jackson began.

"But you lack the means to purchase the book," Sir Shaw finished for him.

Jackson looked down at his feet. "It didn't occur to me that I'd need money when I fell into a pile of hair."

"Well, perhaps we can work out an exchange of gifts."

"What do you mean?"

"I happen to enjoy crossword puzzles a great deal," Sir Shaw explained, "but I am rather perplexed at the moment. Perhaps if you are able to figure out the clue, I could give you the book in exchange?"

Jackson swallowed. He didn't do well on brainteasers. Crosswords made him break out in a sweat. Tests made him woozy. Fill-in-the-blank questions required a lie down. And pop quizzes? Projectile vomiting.

"You could just read a book on deciphering puzzles." Sweat formed on Jackson's upper lip. He wiped it surreptitiously. (*Surreptitiously* is like when you have a booger on your face, and your friend points it out in a kind way, and you casually reach up and flick it away. Unless of course your friend points it out and laughs so you flick the booger on him instead. But that's not surreptitious anymore.)

"That is an excellent idea, sir, but the **Ask** books are not for me. They are for visitors only," he explained, his white tufts of hair dancing lightly.

"Okay, well, I'll do my best." Jackson's stomach gave a nervous twitch. This could get ugly.

Sir Shaw opened his crossword puzzle book and cleared his throat. Jackson caught a glimpse of its complicatedness, in the many columns of teeny-tiny print. Jackson nervously wiped his forehead. His mouth dried out. Oh dear.

"The word has five letters and ends with an L. The clue is, 'slow as a - - - - - l.'"

Jackson's head spun and his stomach churned. He could still feel last night's bean burgers down there. He swallowed thickly.

"Snail?" he whispered.

Sir Shaw's body convulsed briefly. His breath was ragged as he placed his long fingers over his eyes. He reached into his green blazer pocket and pulled out a black silk handkerchief and patted his forehead. He looked down at the cross-word puzzle, his bushy white eyebrows covering his dark blue eyes.

"That seems to be the answer. No wonder ..." and Sir Shaw shuddered violently again.

"Are you all right?" asked Jackson.

"Yes. I just (*shudder*) do not care for snails," Sir Shaw whispered, smoothing his white hair tufts. They lay flat for a moment and then popped up again.

"What's so bad about snails?"

"The reasons I do not care for them involves a shipwreck, a roll of toilet paper, and a poorly written synopsis, but we will not discuss that right now." He gave Jackson a small smile. "I think we have an agreement, then. You may take the book. Thank you for your help." Sir Shaw turned and walked away.

Jackson smiled to himself as he walked over and sat down in the big, green, overstuffed comfy chair. Meeka slept in the chair beside him. She snorted loudly, rolling over. Her head hung off the cushion, and her long, messy hair touched the floor.

Jackson took a deep breath and opened the book.

There was absolutely nothing written in it.

Jackson turned the pages frantically.

Nothing.

Clean, pure white pages of nothingness stared back at him.

"Are you kidding me?" Jackson yelled. Meeka snorted again, but didn't move. Jackson flipped through the pages furiously ... all blank.

What? He had gone through all of that ... that stress! The sweating! The nausea! He had almost thrown up! And for what? A stupid book with nothing written in it?

Jackson jerked himself out of the chair (which took a few tries as it was a very thick cushiony seat), and stomped over to the **ASK** section.

But the **ASK** section had disappeared.

Jackson looked wildly around him.

Gone.

He clomped over to the counter and banged his fist on the well-polished silver bell. It tinged an annoyed ting, as though offended.

Sir Shaw stepped out from behind the deep maroon velvet curtain.

"May I help you, sir?" he asked in a very serious voice that was also very dignified and very polite.

Jackson slammed the book on the counter between them.

"There's nothing in this book! I got ripped off!"

Sir Shaw looked at the book on the counter, and then fixed his dark blue eyes on Jackson.

"And what is it exactly that you were looking for, sir?" he asked, one bushy white eyebrow arching.

Jackson exploded. "I wasn't *looking* for anything! *You* sent me to the **ASK** section and *you* offered me a trade and I got ripped off! There is nothing in this book! It's empty! I helped you, and I got nothing in return! I almost threw up!"

Sir Shaw glanced down at the book again. "Nothing is in it at all, sir?"

"No! Nothing is in it at all!"

Sir Shaw looked at Jackson quietly. Jackson felt a little embarrassed about his behavior. But he was still very angry. He took a deep breath and let it out slowly. Sir Shaw reached his hand out toward the book, but his fingers didn't touch it.

"Perhaps there is a reason why there is nothing written in it, sir."

Jackson stared back at him, fuming.

"Now if you will excuse me, I do not believe I can help you any further in this matter." And he slipped behind the deep maroon velvet curtain, his crossword puzzle tucked under his arm.

"Are you kidding me? That's it? What am I supposed to do with a book that has nothing in it? Hey! If I wanted a journal, I would have looked for a journal! I wasn't *looking* for anything!"

He stomped over to Meeka and nudged her. Meeka shot up like a startled cat and jumped behind her chair.

"I'm not doing anything wrong!" she yelled looking wildly around. Then she noticed Jackson. She straightened up, wiping the whipped cream off her chin.

"Oh, are you ready to go?" she asked, patting her wispy hair back in place.

Jackson gave a jerky nod. "There's nothing for me here," he said. And he stomped out the door.

Meeka slung her tour-guide bag over her shoulder, and her big, brown eyes spotted the brown book on the well-polished counter. She quickly glanced around and then snatched the book, shoving it into her worn, bulging tour-guide bag. She ran out the door.

The deep maroon velvet curtain twitched and a set of dark blue eyes with bushy, white eyebrows over them disappeared from view. Then there was a soft chuckle.

In Which There Is Frustration, Annoyance, Irritation, and Exasperation

Jackson was being a crabby-crabber-ton. Can you blame him? He was frustrated, annoyed, irritated, infuriated, exasperated, enraged, perturbed, and discouraged. He was even a little bit hungry. Hmm ... perhaps the hunger had something to do with the crabbiness? Obviously he was frustrated, annoyed, irritated, infuriated, exasperated, enraged, perturbed, and discouraged because of the whole book incident, but don't things always look better after you eat? They say that things will look better in the morning and this too shall pass, but seeing as how Jackson could not wait until morning to finish his tour, perhaps eating would help.

Let's continue with the story and hope that Jackson eats soon because no one wants to read a book with a cranky character. Actually, you may be feeling a bit peck-ish yourself right now. So if you want to go get something to eat, I don't mind waiting for you. After all, no one likes a cranky reader.

chapter

17

In Which We Find a Doorknob

As they walked down the corridor, Jackson felt a little tired. And a little hungry. As delicious as bean burgers are, they just don't keep a person satisfied for long.

"Meeka, is there somewhere we can get something to eat?"

She looked up at him then tripped and fell on her face. Her tour-guide bag slapped down on the floor, spilling its contents everywhere. Meeka quickly grabbed the plain brown book and shoved it back inside, along with the dead, smelly fish.

"Are you okay?" Jackson bent down to help her. "Meeka, why do you have a fish in your ... hey look at that!" Jackson sat back and stared. "Is that a ... a doorknob?"

Meeka looked mystified. "It sure looks like one."

It was indeed a doorknob.

In the middle of the floor.

Huh.

Jackson debated turning the doorknob. He didn't see a door there, but why else would there be a doorknob in the middle of the floor? Jackson touched the doorknob. He turned it an eighth of an inch ... then a quarter inch ... then...

"Oh, look! We're here!" Meeka cried. She quickly jammed the rest of her spilled items into the bag.

Jackson looked up. Sure enough, there in the corridor in front of them was a big orange door with a sign on it.

THE CAFETERIA

"Come on, Jackson!" Meeka stood up and adjusted her tour-guide bag.

Jackson hesitated. He really wanted to see what was beneath the doorknob on the floor. But he really wanted to see what was in the cafeteria as well. And what was with the dead fish? His stomach argued with his curiosity. Don't you hate it when your body parts argue with each other?

"Okay, but we'll have to come back here, though."

And into the cafeteria they went.

chapter 18

In Which We Visit the Cafeteria

You think you know what cafeterias are like. With their white walls and faded posters of large, smiling faces eating shiny, red apples. With strange smells seeping from badly scratched dishes making you nauseous and hungry at the same time. And the lunch lady with the huge hairy wart on her chin serving up wilted French fries, congealed baby corn, and perfectly cubed carrots. The crusty-edged, overcooked hamburgers in stale buns are stuck to the pans, and the green-brown pudding seems to be moving. The dining tables have broken benches and their broken wheels always trip you.

That is absolutely nothing like the cafeteria that Jackson and Meeka walked into.

"Wow, this is absolutely nothing like any cafeteria I've ever walked into!" Jackson exclaimed in wonder. "Granted, I've never been in a cafeteria in my great-aunt's hair either."

The walls were painted a warm, inviting yellow. The same color as the melted butter you pour over your hot popcorn before you sit down to watch a good movie.

Instead of broken benches, there were small circular tables with bright red-checkered tablecloths. Black wrought-iron chairs circled them. Each red-checkered table was set for two, with tall, extravagant menus standing up at each place setting. Meeka led Jackson over to a table and they sat down. Jackson picked up a tall, extravagant menu and opened it.

The glossy black pages were blank save for a few words written in gold script:

"Whatever I want?" asked Jackson.

The Author invites you to ask for whatever you want

"Whatever you want," repeated Meeka.

"Meeka, who is this author? Is it Tolkien?"

"Um ..." and she was interrupted.

A waiter materialized at their table. (He didn't *actually* materialize. He actually came out from the swinging door behind the counter, but they hadn't seen him.)

The waiter's head resembled a large potato and had thinning black hair slicked against his pink scalp. His black caterpillar eyebrows met in the middle of his forehead, forming a straight line over his cauli- flower nose. He had thick lips and a teeny-tiny black moustache. His tuxedo was very black and very tight. The buttons strained dangerously. His thick sausage fingers held a shiny silver tray.

"An what weel you be 'aving today, sir?" the waiter boomed with a heavy French accent.

"What do you have?" asked Jackson.

"We 'ave whatehvair you want," the waiter sniffed imperiously.

"Whatever I want?"

"Zat ees what I say. Whatehvair you want."

"But I don't know what I want."

"Zen I cannot get you ennyseeng, can I?"

"Can I think about it for a moment?"

"Oui." The French waiter yanked a chair from an adjacent table and sat down right next to Jackson. His chair creaked as he leaned back, folding his hands across his vast stomach. His black shiny buttons strained against his vest. A big sausage finger scratched his puny little moustache and began to pick his nose.

Jackson looked at Meeka nervously. "What are you going to eat?"

Meeka shrugged. "I've already tried everything, so I'll just have what you're having."

"What do people usually order?" Jackson asked the rotund waiter.

The waiter's beady black eyes looked at him steadily. "Zey ordair what zey need to eat."

"What they *need* to eat? That doesn't make any sense."

The waiter huffed. "Pouf! Zat ees a reedeekulous seeng to say. Of course eet make sense."

"Well, can you explain it to me?" asked Jackson.

The waiter's shiny black buttons strained.

"Please?"

The waiter blinked slowly and toyed with his moustache.

"All right" he said graciously (see how important it is to mind your manners?). "You ordair what you need. Zome peepel, zay need lots of courage, so zay ordair prime rib weeth thick sausage gravy and garleek mashed potatoes."

"Of course," murmured Jackson. "But I don't eat meat, you see."

The waiter's chest puffed a little bigger. His French face turned pink. "Bah, *qu'est-ce que vous me dites*? From whair else do you get your courage?"

Jackson shrugged. "I don't know. What else do people order?"

The waiter sulked. "Zome peepel 'oo need lots of energie, zay ordair wheat pasta weeth sausage and sliced zucchini and parmesan."

"What if someone wanted to do well on a test?" Jackson quizzed.

"Feesh, of course! *C'est bon, le poisson!* Greelled salmon weeth steamed green beans een thyme-butter!" the waiter sniffed.

"And what if someone wants to make friends?"

"Nahsing weeth garleek, of course."

Jackson thought for a moment. "And what if one were to embark on an adventure?"

The waiter slicked back his thinning hair, his pinky ring twinkling.

"Zen I recommens a greelled shrimp angel hair pasta weeth asparagus and mushrooms in a light garleek cream sauce weeth a few chilies. So," he sniffed, lifting his bulk out of his chair, "you weel be requiring zee meal of adventure?"

Jackson shrugged. "It's just a tour. Maybe I don't need it at all."

"*Quoi?!*" A shiny black button exploded off the waiter's chest and dented the wall. "Zen you weel stop wasting my time and 'ave zee buffet," he growled, whipping the menus from their hands with his big

70

sausage fingers. He stomped away, smashed the menus on the bar counter, and disappeared behind the swinging door.

Jackson just sat there, a bit confused and a little dumbfounded. That didn't mean that Jackson was dumb or he was becoming dumber. He just didn't know what to say or think in that particular situation. So he said nothing.

Meeka stood up, pulling Jackson's hand eagerly. "Come on, I love the buffet."

Jackson followed Meeka to the other side of the cafeteria to a long table of assorted foods. Meeka grabbed a black-and-white-checkered tray and shoved it into Jackson's hands.

Oh . . .

   . . . my

      . . . goodness.

In Which There Is a Lot of Meat

I want you to take a moment and imagine the longest table you've ever seen. Imagine this superlong table is filled, I mean, fiiiillllllllleddddddd with food. Every kind of food you can imagine. How on earth are you possibly going to decide?

"How on earth am I possibly going to decide?" said Jackson half to himself, half to Meeka.

Meeka shrugged. With skill born of practice she sauntered down the buffet, selected a few things, placed them on her tray and returned to their table.

Jackson approached the buffet table cautiously.

There was meat.

A lot of meat.

You can't begin to understand how much meat there was.

There was grilled steak, broiled beef brisket, barbequed sirloin, rare tenderloin, chuck roast, mushroom hamburgers, fried pork chops, apricot pork tenderloin, grilled pork, stewed pig's feet (eww!), boiled pig snout in apple-brandy sauce (double ewww!), barbecued ribs in thick fig-garlic sauce, lamb curry, broiled rack of lamb, lamb stew, goat stew (you really should try it sometime), deer meat, bear meat, foie gras, pâté, fried duck feet (I think I'm going to be sick), chicken breast, chicken legs, chicken thighs, whole

roasted chicken, twice-fried chicken wings, campfire pheasant, barbecued teriyaki kangaroo ... you name it. If it was meat, it was there.

Jackson hovered for a moment. Then in a frenzied fit, he grabbed a piece of everything.

I mean

E-

   VER-

     Y-

        THING.

His tray was very heavy when he finished.

Jackson shuffled over to the table and dumped his tray onto the table, startling Meeka in the process. She looked up at him with buttery carrot mash on the side of her face.

"Jackson, that's a lot of meat," she said with her mouth full.

Actually it sounded like, "Muphmun! Muph a muph mutt!" but I've translated for you. I'm sure you don't have *Thompson's Full-Mouth Translation Book*.

Jackson sat down. "I know, but I never eat this stuff at home, Meeka. I'm not allowed to eat meat or junk food."

Meeka swallowed. "What's junk food?"

"Um, well, it's food that ... well, I guess it's not really good for you."

"Why would you want to eat junk?"

Jackson ignored her question and picked up a large knife. He cut into the steak. The blade slid through the meat and oozed a pool of juiciness onto his plate. He dabbed the steak into the garlic-shrimp sauce and took a bite.

That ... was ... so ... GOOD!

Jackson ate another piece.

And another.

He felt the blood pump in his veins.

Jackson cut a piece of double-fried chicken. The greasy meat slipped on the plate, making it difficult to stab with his fork, so he picked it up with his fingers and popped it into his mouth.

Oh, that was so good.

He felt the chewy batter melt on his tongue. He swallowed.

He felt funny.

Maybe he was just very hungry.

Jackson devoured a piece of deep-fried shrimp. He didn't eat shrimp at home. He didn't eat anything that ate off the bottom of the ocean or anything that carried its house on its back either.

He cut into a piece of greasy bacon. Delicious!

Jackson cleaned his plate. He ate E-V-E-R-Y single piece of meat. He would have licked his plate, but that's just bad manners. His belly poked out under his pajamas. He felt a little full. But there was so much more to try!

Delicious!

Jackson lurched his way to the dessert table, pausing to glance at the salad section. Why bother? He ate salad all the time. It was time to live a little and try new things! He loaded up his tray with sweets, candy, chips, and sour gummies. He sat back down at the table and threw the candy into his mouth.

Meeka stopped eating and stared at Jackson. He was chewing so fast his jar was a blur.

"Um, Jackson?" she said hesitantly.

Jackson's hands and mouth moved with blinding speed. "Muh?"

"Your face is sweating. And you're turning red."

Jackson wiped his face with a cloth napkin. He kept eating.

And then something strange happened.

WARNING: There Is Throw Up in This Chapter!

Jackson opened his mouth wide and ...

"BLUUCUURP!"

Meeka's eyes popped open and her jaw dropped. She had spinach stuck in her bottom teeth.

"Ah, uh ... excuse me," Jackson muttered, very embarrassed.

Usually a good burp makes you feel better. You know when you feel the pressure in your belly and then you burp, and all the smelly air comes out and your stomach deflates? Those are the best kind of burps. They're right up there with the loud ones and the ones you use to recite the alphabet.

But this burp didn't relieve the pain. In fact, Jackson felt very sick. His stomach protruded so much he felt like he was going to throw up ... or maybe explode. Or maybe do both. He rubbed his belly. His face was sweating. His stomach churned and jiggled with nausea, just like when a pop quiz was coming up.

"Ooohhhh, Meeka! I feel so sick!" Jackson groaned.

"Well, I'm not surprised! You didn't eat any salad or greens or fruit at all!" she scolded.

Jackson rubbed his belly faster. His heart pounded in his chest and he felt afraid. He was sick indeed. He had eaten too much, and he had eaten too many of the wrong things. He looked around desperately and spotted a bathroom. He ran to the door and went inside.

I'm not going to tell you what happened in there. It's too awful. If you've ever been sick before, you know exactly what happened in there.

Some time passed. Jackson slowly opened the door and staggered over to Meeka. She clandestinely shoved the plain, brown book back into her tour-guide bag. (*Clandestinely* is like when you try to sneak cookies from the cookie jar without getting caught. I do not approve of such tactics. If you want a cookie, you should ask. If you are told no, I'm sure there are some good reasons, even if you don't like them.)

Everything is permissible ... but not everything is beneficial

Jackson slumped into his chair. His pajamas were wet and his face sickly and pale. He glanced over at the buffet table and felt his stomach churn. Then he noticed a sign on the table.

Why, oh WHY, hadn't he noticed that before? Jackson sighed.

Meeka stood up and patted his head like a dog. "I'll help you feel better, Jackson. Wait here." She left the table for a few moments and then came back with a tray full of food.

Jackson groaned weakly. "Oh, Meeka, I can't eat anything! I'm sick! I'm shaking! My stomach is still churning. I feel like there's a kangaroo jumping in my belly!"

Meeka pushed the tray in front of Jackson. The smell of the food made him nauseous.

"Eat," she said.

"I can't."

"Eat!"

"I can't!"

Meeka speared a baby tomato and tried to shove it into his mouth.

Jackson jerked his head away. "Stop! STOP! I'LL THROW UP ON YOU!"

"Would you please trust me? I *am* the tour guide, you know." She shoved the tomato into his mouth.

Jackson barely held back the nausea. He felt the bile moving up the back of his throat.

But he chewed.

The sweet tomatoey taste exploded in his mouth. It was so ... good. Jackson felt the nausea subsiding. He took a bite of the lettuce and felt his belly calming down. Fresh strawberries, blueberries, cooked carrots in tarragon butter, wilted spinach and mushrooms ... it was amazing. Jackson stopped sweating and the cramps ceased.

"I don't understand. Why do I feel better now?"

Meeka smiled, tucking some hair behind her elf ears. "Jackson, I know I'm still young, and I'll probably just be a tour guide for my entire life. But what I do know is that if you don't take care of your body, it won't take care of you."

Jackson jumped up from the table. He felt fantastic! He felt like he could take on the world!

Or at least a tour in Great-Aunt Harriett's hair.

"Take me to the next room, Meeka!" Jackson cried. Meeka squeaked with laughter, and off they went.

In Which There Is an Important Conversation

"So, Meeka, how long have you been a tour guide?" Jackson asked as they meandered down the hall.

"Um, longer than I should." Meeka began digging in her bag.

"What do you mean?"

"Well, someone in my position would *normally* have been promoted a long time ago." Meeka shook her head and her long hair fell, covering her face.

Jackson stopped walking to look at her. "Can't you complain?"

"Why should I? I'm the one who keeps messing up," she said, looking earnestly at him. She pulled out a broken pen, studied it for a moment, and then shoved it in her pocket.

"Could you change jobs?"

Meeka began walking again. "Oh no! I'd never ask to move. He has great confidence in placing me right where I am." She pulled out a crumpled piece of paper.

"Who?"

"The Author."

"What Author? Lemony Snickett? Is he your boss?"

"Oh yes, but He's so much more than that. He's also my best friend." Meeka pulled out a twisted barrette from her bag. She shoved it back in.

"Lemony Snickett is your best friend?"

Meeka stared at Jackson. "What? No! Who's Lemony Snickett?"

Jackson shook his head, confused. "OK, wait a minute. How could your best friend put you in a job you don't like?"

"We-ell. It's complicated. But not. It's definitely a long story," said Meeka. And she stopped walking because they had arrived at something very unexpected.

You'd think at this point Jackson would stop expecting anything, because so many unexpected things had already happened, and he should have expected the unexpected. But sometimes people don't like unexpected things, and I'm sorry to say, despite Jackson's young age, he had given up expecting the unexpected and preferred to expect the expected. So this was definitely unexpected.

"This is definitely unexpected, Meeka," Jackson said, rather predictably.

It was a door. The door was lovely, but rather out of place. It definitely wasn't the kind of door you'd expect to find in a hallway. (But then, none of the doors were expected.)

It was painted a vivacious red. Hanging on the vivaciously red-painted door was a large, black dragonfly-shaped door knocker.

Meeka smiled mysteriously, her tiny little hand lifting the door knocker and ...

The vivacious red door swung open.

"BOOM!"

ANOTHER WARNING: This Chapter Has Gargantuan, Hairy-Backed Spiders in It!

Jackson and Meeka stepped onto a patch of squishy grass. They were outside. At least, it seemed as though they were outside. The sky was bright blue, birds sang in the distance, and the grass was a lush green. In front of them was a path that led to ...

"What on earth is a whole house doing in here?" Jackson asked, bewildered.

Meeka smiled a little smile. "This house has always been in here."

I'm sure you're wondering if this is for real. I mean, how many rooms or hallways or houses could actually fit into someone's hair? Even someone with very, very, very, very, very, very, very, very, big hair?

I have absolutely no idea. Perhaps Jackson shrank when he went into her hair. Perhaps he passed through a portal to another world. I wasn't given that information, and I was so enthralled with the story when it was told to me, I forgot to ask. Sometimes you get so caught up in something that you forget to ask the right questions. Like when someone has a baby, you are just so excited for them you forget to ask what it is. A boy? A girl? A goldfish? So you'll just have to

accept that this is not my story, I can't answer all the questions, and we'll move on.

Jackson stared at the path.

Well, it was kind of a path. You couldn't really see it for all the weeds.

Yes, weeds. And not the nice kind. These were bad, ugly, dangerous weeds. There were the kind of weeds with sharp thorns. And there were the creep-along-the-ground kind waiting to snatch your ankles. And there were the little, innocent, daisy-like weeds that looked oh-so-cute, but once you were close they reeked of fishy dog breath.

Jackson carefully maneuvered his way along the path, avoiding the perilous weeds. He approached a lovely wrap-around porch. Well, it would have been lovely if not for the chipped white paint exposing gray patches of worn, worm-eaten wood.

There was something very familiar about this house, but he couldn't put his finger on what.

With a fabulous screech, Meeka vaulted onto the porch and began climbing the railing.

Jackson's eyes opened wide as he watched her.

"What are you doing?" he cried. "You could fall and hurt yourself!"

Meeka rolled her big eyes in exasperation. (Go ask your mom what that means. Ask her about twenty times.) "This is the only way in!" And she pulled herself up.

"But what if you fall?" He pointed to the front door. "Look, there's a perfectly good front door to go in! Why don't we just use that?"

Perhaps he shouldn't have said that.

The front door was indeed a perfectly good way to go in.

If you didn't mind the big hole in the floor or the boards nailed across the door.

Or the huge skull-and-crossbones sign with large letters that read "*Go away.*"

Or the wispy cobwebs strung across the railings.

Or the gargantuan, hairy-backed spiders hiding in the corners, waiting for their lunch.

No, if you didn't mind those things at all, then the door was an excellent way to go in.

Meeka rolled her eyes again and exhaled a little bird-y sigh. She reached up and grabbed the rafters of the porch.

"Just give me a boost!"

Jackson was not sure about this. "I'm not sure about this, Meeka!" he called out.

Meeka clambered into the upstairs window. "Come on!" she squeaked, and then disappeared, the dusty curtains falling behind her.

Jackson didn't want to climb the porch rail, nor did he want to climb to the upstairs window. Jackson wasn't used to climbing strange things. He preferred climbing safe things, like stairs and into bed. He thought it might be safer and maybe just a bit easier if he were to walk around the porch and see if perhaps there was another door or an unlocked window. Any other way that didn't involve him climbing up a rotting porch roof. Besides, there is something to be said about respecting other people's property, you know.

Jackson climbed the steps carefully, trying not to disturb the gargantuan, hairy-backed spiders hiding in the corners. He held the spiderweb-covered railing as he climbed around the big hole in the porch floor. Jackson wiped a filthy window with his sleeve. He peeked in.

He couldn't believe what he saw.

chapter 23

A Really Short Chapter

Tell your mom or dad or teacher that you absolutely *have* to read this chapter as you are "racked with suspense" and "will probably *die* if you don't continue." Make sure to use those exact words. If they say no, and you decide to read this chapter in the car, there's a very good chance you will throw up on the seat beside you (or on your little brother if he happens to be sitting next to you). If you decide to read it under the blankets at night with a flashlight, you may be extremely tired in the morning. And if you get caught and this book is taken away along with TV privileges, I hereby refuse all responsibility.

A light glowed faintly inside and a shadow moved slowly across the room. Jackson tapped on the window.

"Hello!"

No answer. Jackson sighed and walked down to the next window. It was dirty too. He looked in and . . .

BANG!

chapter

24

A Rather Long Chapter

Ooh, you might want to read this chapter too.
Jackson jumped back, his heart beating like mad.
The explosive sound ricocheted off the faded red brick
walls of the house. It sounded like a gunshot. And it
sounded close.

Oh, dear.

Gunshots are never pleasant, especially when the
sound is close to you. And *especially* if you are tres-
passing at a house with a huge skull-and-crossbones
sign and large letters that read "*Go away.*"

Jackson slowly stepped back and tiptoed to the end
of the porch. Cautiously, he peeked around the corner.
The rickety porch continued to the back door, but there
was a gate blocking the way. A tall, untrimmed cedar
hedge ran the length of the yard, leading right up to
the gate. Jackson slunk toward the gate. He rattled it
gently. Locked. Jackson tried to slip between the bars,
but he didn't fit. He tried to push his way through the
tall, untrimmed cedar hedge. Most cedar hedges are
effective at their job of keeping people out. And this
particular tall, untrimmed cedar hedge was definitely
doing its job.

Jackson jumped again. Should he call out? Should
he yell, "Don't shoot!" or should he hide? What if the
gun was aimed at him?

BANG!

It was definitely louder and closer this time. Jackson dropped to the porch floor. He couldn't see anything. He shinnied closer to the gate. He peered past the bars at the back door to the house. It was bright red with a lovely brass door knocker and a cocoa mat on the floor that said *Welcome*. You could imagine how welcoming it was. Especially at that moment.

Jackson quickly examined the gate. He couldn't climb it. There wasn't a foothold as the bars ran up and down. The top of the fence was too high for him to reach. The gate had a thick brass lock. He pushed his face into the black bars to look down the cedar hedge. A flash of blue ran by, and then it was gone. Should he yell out?

"Hey!" squeaked a familiar voice. "You're supposed to stay with the tour!"

Meeka's head hung out of the window upstairs. Her long brown hair had bits of fluff in it. She looked cross.

"You *have* to stay with the tour! I don't want to get into trouble again!"

"What trouble?"

Meeka's big brown eyes disappeared as she ducked back inside.

"What trouble, Meeka?" he called up to her. "Meeka? What trouble?"

BANG!

It was very close this time.

Incredibly close.

Scarily close.

Nerve-rackingly close.

It was really close. Let's just leave it at that.

"Stop yelling! You're scaring away the crubbies!"

It was a girl's voice. An *angry* girl's voice. Jackson thought about running away.

"Excuse me!" he called out instead. "Can I please talk to you?"

It was very quiet.

Eerily quiet.

You couldn't hear anything because it was so quiet.

Why was it still so quiet?

BANG!

"What do you want? I'm busy!" the girl's voice yelled.

"Please, I want to talk to you!" Jackson called.

Footsteps pounded the ground, pounded the steps of the porch, and then she was in front of him, the iron gate separating them.

The girl's long, dirty-blonde hair was tucked behind her elf-like ears. Her big brown eyes bore into him. Her blue uniform shirt was dirty.

Her blue combat pants were dirty.

And her boots?

You bet. Dirty.

Jackson was nervous. And he had every reason to be nervous because this angry girl held a gun in her dirty hands.

A very big gun.

A rifle, in fact.

Oh, dear.

She reached up and brushed her dirty-blonde hair impatiently from her eyes. "What do you want? I'm very busy!"

Jackson smiled a little trying to ease the situation. "That's a very nice gun you have there. Are you hunting?"

The girl looked over her shoulder and then looked back at him. "Yes, it is a nice *rifle*. My father gave it to me. He's one of the best hunters in the whole world. His name is Deek Sodo. I assume you've heard of him?"

Jackson shook his head. "I'm not from around here. I'm on a tour."

The girl looked up at the house, one eyebrow arched. "Let me guess. You're on a tour with Meeka."

"Yeah. How did you know that?"

The girl frowned at Jackson. "You're not supposed to be here, you know."

They both looked up at the window. Two big brown eyes ducked behind a curtain.

"Meeka! You're not *supposed* to bring people here on the tour! You're going to get fired! And you're going to make me look bad!" the angry girl yelled.

Jackson looked at the girl in surprise. "You know Meeka?"

"Of course I know her. She's my little sister. I'm Rayaa."

"So, what are you hunting?" he asked.

"I'm hunting crubbies. I used to do tours like Meeka, but then I was promoted to Hunter. But, I never brought anyone here because it's NOT PART OF THE TOUR!" she yelled at the window.

Meeka's little head poked out again.

"You might as well as come down! You can't possibly get into more trouble than you are now!" Rayaa called.

Meeka's head disappeared and a boot popped out, followed by a little leg covered by a frayed hem. Meeka crawled out of the window and jumped, landing on the ground beside Rayaa. Rayaa slung her rifle over one shoulder and began to groom Meeka's wild hair, tying it back into a neater ponytail. She pulled out a large piece of orange fluff.

"Are you enjoying the tour?" Rayaa asked Jackson, conversationally.

"Uh ... I am so far. I think I saw someone in the house, though. I banged on the window, but no one answered."

Rayaa nodded at him, pulling a piece of hay from Meeka's hair. "That's Eliessa. She's a Reader. That's her job. My job is to hunt crubbies."

Jackson stared at her. "What's a crubbie?"

She eyed him skeptically. "Are you from another planet or something?"

Jackson didn't get to answer.

"Crubbies are annoying little creatures that always bother the birds in the sanctuary. That's what I guard here, the bird sanctuary. But the crubbies are awful. They sneak in and mess up the birds' nests, pull their

95

feathers, and even blow bubblegum bubbles in their faces!"

"Crubbies chew gum?" Jackson asked, confused.

"Oh yes. And that bothers the birds you see, because they can't." She repositioned the rifle in her hands. Meeka's hair was ... slightly neater. Rayaa's head whipped around.

"There's another one! Come on!" And she took off down the path.

Meeka bent down and lifted the welcome mat, snatching up a key. She unlocked the gate.

"Come on! This part is so much fun!" And she ran after Rayaa.

Jackson ran down the back porch steps and turned toward the cedar hedge, but he didn't know which way they had gone.

BANG!

Meeka's giggle carried to Jackson. He tried to follow her voice, but wouldn't you know it? The cedar hedge was a maze. Do you know of any big cedar hedges outside of secret houses that *aren't* mazes?

So now Jackson was in a maze.

BANG!

Jackson decided to run. But there were so many twists and turns that Jackson's head began to twist and turn.

Stay focused.

He was very tired of running in circles, and he was very, very thirsty.

BANG!

Jackson ran around a corner and ...

In Which There Is a Bathroom Break

I am going to take a bathroom break, so I suggest you do so as well. Holding your bladder for a long time is not very good for you. Make sure you are very quiet, though. Your mom might hear that you are upstairs reading, and she might remember that she has housework for you to do. If you're in bed reading this under the covers with a flashlight, be quiet when you tiptoe to the bathroom. If your parents are reading this to you, and it's past your bedtime, perhaps they will be the **BEST PARENTS IN THE WORLD!** and let you stay up to finish. And then, being the **BEST PARENTS IN THE WORLD**, they'll let you stay home tomorrow to sleep in. And when you wake up at noon, you'll get to reread the book with hot buttered toast and a cup of hot chocolate in bed. There are some parents like that.

If you happen to know any, please email me.

chapter 26

In Which Jackson Cannot Believe His Eyes

Jackson could not believe his eyes.

Actually, he could believe his eyes, because he was looking at what he saw. What I meant to say is that what he saw was just simply amazing. So maybe I should just write that instead.

So here it is, rewritten:

Jackson saw something simply amazing.

It was the most beautiful birdcage in the world.

It was about the size of a shed. A regular shed. Not the crazy "I'm building an ark in my backyard!" shed that so many dads dream about building.

The cage had long, golden spindles weaving around the frame. Carvings of moons and stars hung in between the spindles. Golden perches swung to and fro and shining silver bells tinkled as the wind blew.

And the cage was filled with the most amazing birds.

There were so many different kinds! It was like a

psycho-bird aviary. But they were birds that Jackson had never seen before. There were birds that looked like robins, but they were the size of footballs. There were finches, but they were neon pink. There were fluorescent-green wrens. And gold-and-blue-striped chickens. And the songs they were singing! The pink finch opened his beak and the sweetest sound came out as the rest joined in harmony.

The sound filled Jackson with such a longing, he couldn't explain it. It reminded him of a place he knew but had never seen. A place where he was loved. A place where nothing could ever go wrong. A place where he would always be happy. A place with never-ending cups of hot chocolate with extra whipped cream and chocolate sprinkles.

Jackson wanted to climb into that song and just stay there forever.

BANG!

"*I got him!*"

chapter 27

A Very Sticky Chapter

Jackson jumped, snatched out of his reverie. He ran around a corner of the hedge. A little, furry, striped animal lay on the ground. His head was shaped like an aardvark's, but his nose was the color of a bright blueberry.

Rayaa sauntered over, picked him up, and shook him. A piece of pink bubble gum fell out of his mouth. Rayaa pulled the furry creature's face to her own and said, rather sternly, "Stop chewing gum around the birds! It's mean!"

The creature nodded solemnly, and she set him down gently. He waddled off, his fluffy tail tucked between his legs. Rayaa picked up the gum, wadded it into some tissue, and put it in her pocket.

"What was that?" Jackson asked.

"Crubbie!" Rayaa said, tucking her hair behind her ears. "Don't you listen? It's my job to protect the birds, the poor things."

Jackson didn't understand. "I don't understand."

"It's my job to protect the birds from . . ."

". . . the crubbies, yes, I know," finished Jackson. "But how are you protecting the birds by letting the crubbies get away?"

"What do you think I do? Kill them?" she asked indignantly.

"No, no, I just . . . well, yes," Jackson stammered.

Rayaa shook her head angrily. "Tranquilizers. Effect lasts ten seconds. Come with me."

Jackson fell in step with Rayaa. He looked over his shoulder for Meeka, but she had climbed up onto one of the golden perches of the cage and was stroking a blue chicken. She squeaked at it. It seemed to be enjoying the chin scratch.

"Crubbies are very mischievous," Rayaa began. "They know that the birds can't chew gum. So they blow bubbles in the birds' faces."

"Why do the birds want to chew gum?" Jackson asked.

Rayaa looked at him strangely. "Don't you like to chew gum?"

"Well, of course I do."

"Do you think you're the only one in the world who likes to chew gum? Honestly!" Rayaa tossed her hair. "Anyway, they blow bubbles in the birds' faces, and it vexes the birds. It frustrates them to the point of trying to chew gum themselves, when clearly they shouldn't chew gum."

"Why can't they chew gum?"

"This is why," she said, and they stopped in front of a very strange sight.

The strange sight was not the new birdcage that stood before them. It was not the many birds perched within it. What was strange was that they were all eerily quiet. And if you've ever been in the presence of birds, you know that they never shut up. However, what was even stranger, oh yes, even stranger than

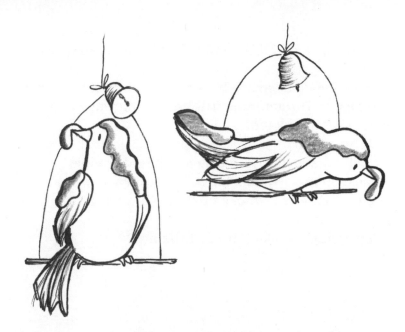

quiet birds, was that the birds were all covered in a weird pink goo.

"Gum," confirmed Rayaa. "These birds gave into temptation and tried to chew a few pieces, poor things. Got gum all over themselves, and their beaks are now stuck. They have to stay here for a few days while I clean them."

"How do you get gum off a bird?"

"With ice cubes and lemon juice of course. Don't you ever get gum stuck in your hair?"

Jackson got a little frustrated with Rayaa, and rightly so. She was smart and sometimes you can get frustrated with smart people because they are just so darn smart.

Jackson changed the subject. "So what do the birds do?"

"They sing, of course!"

"Yes," (he was a little exasperated now), "but why are they in cages?"

"So they can sleep at night! Listen, do you really know so little about birds?"

Jackson changed the subject. "So, Meeka's your sister?"

"Yes, she is. I used to be a tour guide too, but I was promoted to Hunter. She still has a long way to go before she's promoted."

"Why is that?"

"Well ... she always manages to find trouble."

Jackson nodded. Meeka was definitely one of those people ... er, elves, whose curiosity always got the best of them.

A piercing shriek shattered the air.

A Chapter with Lots of Shrieking (Perhaps You Should Put in Earplugs before Continuing)

There are many different kinds of shrieks. There are the quick shrieks, like when someone startles you. And the long shrieks, like when your mom sees a mouse. There is her angry shriek, like when you've left the kitchen a mess, *again*. And there's the sad shriek, like when your dad finds all of his tomato plants uprooted by the dog.

But this was a different shriek.

A loud, horrified shriek.

Jackson and Rayaa ran back toward the beautiful cage with the amazing birds.

It was quite a sight.

The amazing birds were attacking Meeka. Not attacking like they were trying to pluck her eyes out or anything, but they were flying all over her. She shrieked again, waving her arms wildly in the air as a bright pink finch snatched at her hand.

"Meeka! Drop the gum!" Rayaa yelled.

Meeka couldn't hear her for all the birds screeching. Rayaa ran toward the cage, rifle in hand. A crubbie slunk away, a little pink bubble forming on its mouth. Meeka shrieked again.

Rayaa leapt onto the golden perch and knocked
an orange woodpecker off Meeka's arm. She grabbed
Meeka's hand, pried her fingers open, grabbed the
gum, and threw it. The birds squawked angrily.

"Jackson! Hide the gum!"

Jackson didn't think twice. He dove to the ground,
and his fingers snatched the gum as it flew through
the air. He jammed it into his pocket with one smooth
movement. The birds landed and walked toward
Jackson with their wings flared out. They eyed him
suspiciously, their colorful bodies strutting across
the ground as they approached. Jackson opened his
trembling hands, facing them.

"I don't have anything for you."

Jackson made it a habit not to lie. Because lying
is oh-so-very wrong. But Jackson did not want some
umpteen-hundred birds attacking him. So he decided
that it was okay to lie. Just this one time.

"I don't have it. See? Not in my hands!" Technically
he wasn't lying. The gum wasn't in his hands.

A large, yellow pheasant, the size of a fat dog,
waddled over to him, his tail flaring out angrily. His
sharp pointy beak was an inch from Jackson's hands.
Jackson trembled a little, but kept his hands still.
The sharp pointy beak moved to Jackson's nose, the
large, yellow eyes glaring at him. And with a wet snort,

the bird turned away, squawking loudly at the other birds. They all waddled away, chattering to each other. Jackson's heart stopped pounding.

"Whoop! Good catch, Jackson!" Rayaa called out. Jackson pulled the gum out of his pocket and looked at it in wonder. It *was* a good catch. Huh.

"Meeka, you know better than to tease the birds!" Rayaa scolded.

Meeka sulked, sucking on the ends of her hair. Her brown bangs fell into her eyes as she stared at the ground.

"I just wanted some gum for myself. I wasn't giving them any. They just happened to be there when I opened it," Meeka pouted.

Rayaa frowned and then hugged Meeka tightly, "Meeka, you *need* to stop getting into trouble."

Meeka nodded solemnly at her, "I know, Rayaa."

Rayaa turned to Jackson. "Thanks for helpin', Jackson. I really appreciate it. Sometimes it's hard to take care of two sisters, you know."

"Two sisters? There's another one?"

Rayaa nodded her head at the house. "Eleissa is in there. You saw her reading inside. That's her job. She reads."

Jackson shrugged, unimpressed. "Anyone can read."

Rayaa smiled mysteriously. "Ah yes, but Eleissa can read anything."

"So what? I can read anything too." (Actually he couldn't read French, but we won't get into that right now.)

Rayaa smiled even more mysteriously. "Yes, but Eleissa can read things that haven't even been written yet!"

She glanced up at the sky. "Well, it's getting late, and I have to go. I'm sure there are a lot more crubbies, around and I need to do my job." She looked pointedly at Meeka.

Meeka smiled a little smile from under her bangs. Rayaa pulled her aside and began speaking quietly to her. Jackson couldn't hear exactly what they were saying, but he heard, "key ... door ... garden shed" and then, very distinctly, "put that fish back!"

Meeka nodded and hugged Rayaa. Rayaa surreptitiously kissed her on the head. (I've already explained this word, but just in case you've forgotten ... *surreptitiously* is like when your little sister is holding an ice cream cone and you lick it when no one is looking.) She turned and walked away. Meeka straightened her uniform and approached Jackson.

"Shall we continue?" she asked, very businesslike.

29

In Which There Is a Great Deal of Important Talk. Also, Feathers.

What were you guys talking about?" asked Jackson as they came closer to the hedge entrance.

"Oh. Um. Nothing." Meeka glanced down at her fingernails for a moment then flashed Jackson a charming smile. "Shall we go in through the back door?"

"Do you do a lot of tours here?" Jackson asked as they began walking.

"Oh, I get enough work," Meeka reached up and pulled a huge yellow feather out of her hair.

"How is all of this happening in my Great-Aunt Harriett's hair?" Jackson reached up and pulled a pink feather out of his own hair. "I mean, I know I saw her put a dog in her hair once, during a tornado, but ... do people really just climb in?"

"We-ell, there are many different ways to get here," she said as she reached up and pulled a green feather out of Jackson's hair.

"How is that possible? Do people just trip and fall into her hair all the time?" Jackson gestured wildly as he spoke. A blue feather fell from his hair.

"No, no, no, no. We're in your aunt's hair, right?"

"Right ..."

"But we're not."

"What?"

"Try to see it this way," Meeka began as she pulled an orange feather from her hair. "We aren't in Great-Aunt Harriett's hair anymore. We are ... we're on the Author's Tour."

"Yes, you've told me that. But which author? C.S. Lewis? He was a great writer."

"No, no, no, no. Not that kind of author." Meeka reached up and pulled a white feather out of her hair.

"I don't understand any of this. What are you talking about?" Jackson reached up and pulled a violet feather out of her hair.

"What don't you understand? It's *the* Author."

Jackson sighed. He reached up and pulled a red feather out of his hair. (That seemed to be the last of the feathers.) He tried a different approach. "So, does everyone go on the Author's Tour?"

"Only if they want to," Meeka said, and they climbed the steps to the back door of the house. Because they had walked, all the way back, to the back door of the house.

"But I never knew about it until I fell in!" Jackson protested. He really didn't understand. And he reached up, again, and pulled a black feather out of Meeka's hair. (Apparently that hadn't been the last of the feathers.)

Meeka smiled mischievously. "Weren't you lured by the idea of an adventure? Didn't you think you'd have the chance to be a hero?"

Jackson stopped in his tracks and turned red. "Wait, how did you ..."

"We're here!" she chirped happily.

In Which We Need a Key. Do You Happen to Have One We Could Borrow?

It was a lovely door. Such a door is a door that everyone should have on their house; unless, of course, you never want visitors. Which is how I feel sometimes, but we won't get into that right now.

Meeka lifted up the mat to get the key.

Oh dear ... no key.

"Oh dear! No key!" exclaimed Meeka.

Jackson felt his pockets. "I didn't take it."

Meeka sighed heavily, her brows furrowing in concentration and worry. "Well, I'm not going to bother Rayaa."

Meeka's little hand reached up and grabbed the handle of the huge brass knocker, lifting it. Jackson saw her hand tremble.

Meeka swallowed loudly.

The knocker dropped.

BOOOOOOOOOOOMMMMMMMMMMM!

"Gaaargh!" Jackson clapped his hands over his ears.

"That'll get her attention!"

113

"WHAT?" He could only hear the ringing in his ears. Meeka pulled his ear to her mouth.

"THAT'LL GET HER ATTENTION!" she yelled.

"Whose attention?" he asked, rubbing his ears.

"Eleissa's!"

The big, red, welcoming door opened.

chapter 31

In Which We Meet a Scowl

A little scowling face with bright blue eyes stared at them.

"There *is* a key, you know," the little scowling face with bright blue eyes said.

"Elcissa, this is Jackson. I'm taking him on the Tour," Meeka announced.

Eleissa looked Jackson up and down. She covered her face with a large book. "I'm busy. Doing my *job*." Her piercing blue eyes stole a peak over the top of the book.

Meeka giggled uncomfortably. "Eleissa, I'm giving him the Tour. You know. The Author's Tour?" She waggled her eyebrows at her.

Eleissa looked up briefly and scowled again. "You're interrupting my reading," she said. And with that, she spun around and walked into the house, leaving the door wide open.

Jackson heard her mumbling as she stomped down the hall, "NOT supposed to

make the HOUSE part of the TOUR! Mumble, mumble
... AGREEMENT."

Meeka slipped inside and motioned for Jackson to
follow her.

A Chapter That Has
Many Portraits

The inside of the hallway was lovely. But what would you expect with such a welcoming door? If the hallway was dark, dirty, and dank, wouldn't you be oh-so disappointed?

The walls were painted bright ultramarine blue with red trim. A chandelier hung from the ceiling, casting little rainbows about as the sunshine tickled the crystals.

Meeka knocked her dirty boots on the welcoming welcome mat and walked ahead. Jackson knocked his dirty shoes and noticed that his pajamas were dusty. He brushed his legs as best as he could. He took his dusty glasses off and large tufts of his great-aunt's hair shoved into his face. Jackson took a deep breath, carefully of course, so as not to inhale any hair, and polished the glasses on the front of his shirt. He slowly put the glasses back on. He could see again. The hair had magically moved away.

Little red tables lined the blue walls. Jackson stopped at the first one. The red table was old-fashioned with carved legs and had an ornate door handle that opened a little drawer. Sitting on top of the red table was a calligraphy pen. Jackson picked it up carefully, marveling at the weight in his hand. It fit perfectly. He unscrewed the top to examine its delicate nib. If this part is boring to you, it is because you have not yet learned to appreciate the fine quality workmanship of expensive calligraphy pens.

Jackson put the pen back with a longing sigh. Despite his young age, he could appreciate a fine pen. He glanced up at a mirror mounted in an old gilt frame that was hanging above the red table. Jackson looked into it and saw his very dirty nose. He wiped it self-consciously on his arm. His hair was messy, sticking up everywhere. He smoothed it down, but to no avail. The frame held a tiny brass plate with an inscription. Jackson looked closer. It read, "Zero". *Well that doesn't make any sense*, he thought.

He stopped at the next table, bending over to admire the little angel figurines on it "that we're not allowed to touch," Meeka explained. Her little hands twitched beside him and he knew she was just dying to touch them. She cleared her throat and, with great restraint, stepped away. Jackson stood up and glanced into the mirror hanging on the wall above this table.

Except it wasn't a mirror this time, but a portrait. Well, not a portrait but a group picture. A group picture of baseball players. The player in the front row had a big grin on his face as he held a trophy. Jackson peered closer and ...

Wh-at?

It was him!

But it wasn't him!

Jackson shook his head and looked again.

Sure enough, it was him.

But it wasn't him.

It was Jackson, but older. About ten years older. The twenty-and-a-half-year-old Jackson grinned broadly, clutching the trophy. He was taller, broader in the shoulders and ... he was the captain of the team? Jackson looked at the other players in the picture. They were all smiling. He looked back at himself. Wow. On the gold frame was another brass plate with an inscription. It read: *Ten*. Ten what?

"How on earth could that be me? That's ridiculous!" Jackson's mind went a mile a minute. (That's one point six kilometers a minute, for you metric folk.)

Jackson didn't know what to think. He looked at the next picture.

It had another gold frame with another little sign, but it read: *Forty*. Jackson peered intently at the group shot. Fifteen people, all about forty years old, sat in three rows. They wore important-looking, official blazers.

Behind them was a university banner. Jackson scanned the faces looking back at him.

There he was! Wow. He was old!

He had graying hair and eyes that were starting to crinkle around the edges. He even had a moustache! Jackson laughed out loud. He was a teacher! Jackson remembered how his classmates laughed at him when he told them he wanted to be a teacher. His teachers told him he had to work harder, to study more, and to quit daydreaming for goodness' sakes!

Jackson . . . a teacher. Wow.

"Meeka, what are these?" he asked quietly, still staring at the pictures.

She turned and walked back to him. "Oh, those are just the future mirrors."

"Future mirrors? This isn't a mirror; it's a portrait!"

"They mirror who you will be later on."

"So that's me?"

Meeka shrugged, unconcerned. "If that's what you see, then that's what you are."

Jackson ran to the next mirror, nearly knocking Meeka over in his haste.

"Hey!"

Jackson was shocked by the next mirror. The little sign in the gold frame read: *Sixty*. The man in the portrait was old. His white hair was slicked down and he had deep wrinkles on his gentle, friendly face. It was Jackson's face. A very *old* Jackson. The very old Jackson was shaking hands with someone important-looking. The prime minister? A flag stood upright on a pole beside them. A banner hung over the figures shaking hands for the camera. It read, *Thompson Award*. Jackson laughed out loud. One only received the Thompson Award after writing something completely brilliant, such as *Thompson's Full-Mouth Translation Book*. Imagine! Who was the daydreamer now?

Wait. Was this real?

Was this really Jackson's story?

"Jackson! Let's go! I thought you wanted a tour!"

"But Meeka look! Look at me!"

She looked into the mirror. "I don't see anything."

Jackson looked back. "But it's me! Don't you see? It's me! Look, I'll show you!" And he dragged her down to the first mirror.

"Look, here's me right now. Plain, old, boring ten-and-a-half-year-old Jackson. Now look at the next one!" Jackson dragged her down the hall.

"This is me later on. Look at me! I've got a beard! Well, kind of."

"Um," said Meeka.

"And look!" cried Jackson, ignoring her. "I'm captain of the baseball team! And look at this one!" He pulled her farther down the hallway.

"Look! I'm a professor at the University! Look at me! And in this one down here ... look at how OLD I am! But look what's in my hands! I've won the Thompson Award! This is my story, Meeka!"

Meeka shook her head. "Jackson, I can't see any of that."

Jackson whipped around. "What do you mean? Why can't you see my story?"

"Because it's your future, not mine."

"But ... but this is real, right? These are mirrors of the future? This is going to happen, right?"

Meeka didn't answer.

Jackson looked back at the mirrors. A flash of inspiration struck him: he was going to write down his story so he could remember it.

"Meeka! Have you got some paper or something I can write on?"

Meeka chewed on her bottom lip as she searched her tour guide bag. She pulled out the plain brown book and handed it to him.

"I took this from The Book Room. You left it behind."

Jackson looked at the cover. *How to Be Yourself.* He had forgotten. His fingers trailed the smooth cover.

Jackson reached into his satchel and pulled out the pen. He opened the Book to the first page.

There was writing in it.

chapter 33

In Which Jackson Wonders if He's Losing His Mind

Jackson snapped the Book shut.

Was he going crazy?

Jackson read the front cover. Yup, same book.

He took a breath.

He opened the Book.

The first page had one sentence. *You are strong.*

Jackson's heart pounded. Was that ... about him?

It couldn't be about him. He wasn't strong at all! In fact, he was the smallest kid in his class. He ...

Jackson closed the Book again and studied the cover. *How to Be Yourself.* Holding his breath, he opened it again and turned to the second page.

You are a good baseball player.

No he wasn't!

Jackson looked up at the baseball picture. His twenty-year-old self smiled back.

Maybe he was.

Maybe he would be. He turned the page.

You are smart.

Was he smart? University professors had to be smart. And if he was going to win the Thompson Award? Jackson turned the page.

You are an amazing writer.

Next page. *You have a good heart.*

Next page. *You are a good friend.*

What if it was true? What if all of it was true?

Perfect. He would remember and treasure this. He didn't have to write anything down. It was already written out for him. He wouldn't forget.

Jackson tucked the Book into his leather satchel and followed Meeka down the hall.

chapter

34

In Which Nothing Particularly Important Happens

They walked slowly down the hall. Jackson was lost in the loveliness of his thoughts. As for what Meeka was thinking, who knows? I had the opportunity to ask her once what she was thinking, and she replied, "The color red, if daisies would make a good bed, and how to make shoelaces out of molasses."

I never bothered to ask again.

Meeka stopped in front of the ultramarine blue wall. "Here we are!"

chapter

35

In Which Something Small Happens

Jackson looked around. They were in the middle of the hallway. "Here we are, where?"

Meeka rolled her big brown eyes at him. "Here we are at Eleissa's Reading Room, of course!"

chapter 36

In Which There Is Another Room

What would you imagine a reading room looks like? Well, you would imagine a reading room to look like The Book Room right? With a huge fireplace and a cheery fire; bookshelves filled with books; large, comfy, squashy chairs; dark wood paneling; and a lovely place where you could put your feet up and drink hot chocolate with extra whipped cream and chocolate sprinkles, right?

This was not the case at all. No huge fireplace with a cheery fire, no bookshelves with books, no large, comfy, squashy chairs, and no dark wood paneling.

Instead, dark purple curtains hung on the walls. On the walls, if you can imagine! There was only one window, and it was dirty, save for the smudged mark Jackson had made. The room was completely bare.

Except for the large, brown tent in the middle of the room.

In Which We Learn about the Book, the Author, and Fred the Turtle

An eerie light glowed within the tent, casting strange shadows on the walls.

Meeka lifted the flap. "Eleissa, we've come to visit you!"

There was no answer.

"Eleiiiiiiiiiiiiiisaaaa!" she sang.

A loud irritated sigh came from within the tent. "I told you that I'm reading!"

"But I want you to meet Jackson!"

"I've already met him."

Meeka climbed into the tent, the flap closing behind her. Jackson heard angry little whispers and then a pleading voice.

Then quiet.

The tent flap opened.

"Well, come in then," the grouchy voice said.

Jackson pulled back the flap and climbed in.

It was a nice setup actually. Especially for a tent. A huge, comfy-looking, orange sleeping bag lay on the floor. It was surrounded by purple cushions edged in gold trim. A battery-operated lantern hung from the middle of the tent, softly lighting the inside. Eleissa sat scrunched up in the corner, her long hair hanging in her face. She put her book down and looked at Jackson with large, blue, serious eyes.

"So, what do you want to know?" she asked.

Jackson looked at Meeka, who sat with her legs crossed as she chewed on the ends of her long brown hair. Jackson sat beside her, pulling off his satchel.

"Uh ..." Jackson articulated. (*Articulate* is when you're describing something really well. But given Jackson's vocabulary at this moment, the word is actually used in irony. *Irony* is when something opposite of what should happen happens. Like when you find money on the street and then you lose it.)

Eleissa slowly tucked a piece of long blonde hair behind her ear, er, elf ear.

"What should I ask?" he whispered to Meeka.

Eleissa rolled her big blue eyes in exasperation.

"I'm a Reader," she said, as if that explained everything.

But that didn't explain everything, did it? It didn't explain why she was sitting in a tent in the middle of a room or why the window was dirty or why her job was to read. Nor did it explain the cosine of 7.88 or what the word for "couch" was in Spanish.

Jackson just stared at her. Words were not forming in his mouth.

"It means that I read things. I can read anything," she said superciliously. (*Supercilious* is when someone is very arrogant and grouchy. Like when your cat is sleeping on the couch, but then he rolls over and hits the floor, and he stands up and shakes all over? It's the look on his face as he walks away. If you don't have a cat, maybe you could YouTube one or something.)

Jackson looked at Meeka, who nodded very seriously.

"What do you read?"

Eleissa picked up the large book she was holding. It was leather bound with very thick pages. It was the size of an extensive dictionary. Her tiny fingers caressed the pages.

"Right now I'm reading about the progression of a butterfly in our backyard. I want to know if he ends up migrating or not."

"That doesn't sound like a very interesting story," Jackson snorted.

Eleissa flipped her hair off her face. "I'm a Reader. I read and find out what happens. And then I know." She looked at him through lowered eyelashes. "Haven't you ever wanted to know *everything*?" Jackson shrugged. She smiled. "Well, I read and find out. So now I know a lot. I probably know more than you do."

Jackson didn't say anything. She probably knew more than he did, and he wasn't about to get into a big discussion about it.

"Ask me a question, any question," she challenged.

"Okay," he said slowly. "Can you tell me about Fred?" Ha! She wouldn't know anything about Fred.

Eleissa sniffed self-importantly and shook the heavy book slowly in her hand.

She placed the heavy book onto a purple velvet cushion edged in gold trim and gently opened its pages. She looked down at the book and read quietly.

133

"Fred is your turtle. He gets lost next week when you clean his cage, and your little sister finds him and hides him in her dollhouse for three weeks, feeding him broccoli until you find out. You get upset but then realize that this is a great way of getting rid of your broccoli." Eleissa closed the book.

Jackson was amazed. "Wow. I'm amazed."

"I already knew you'd say that."

"What do you mean?"

Eleissa smirked at him. "I've been reading your story."

Jackson was confused. "I'm confused. How can you do that?"

Eleissa picked up the book, shaking it again. She opened the first page.

"Jackson's life—Jackson will be born two weeks late after his mother is in labor for twenty-seven hours."

Eleissa flipped a few pages, continuing in a bored voice.

"Jackson will be the pitcher when he plays baseball today, but every single batter he throws against will hit the ball. They will lose the game. Jackson will be hard on himself."

Jackson's face turned red. "How do you know that? Why is that in there?"

134

Eleissa smiled a Cheshire-cat smile at him. "I told you. I'm a Reader."

Jackson frowned as an awful thought occurred to him.

Eleissa could read every terrible thing that happened to him. She could read about how he lost every baseball game he pitched. How he made his little sister cry when he threw her doll out the window. How he prayed at night for a best friend. Jackson felt frustration creeping up on him. Don't you hate it when things creep up on you? Anger, burps, your dentist appointment.

This was definitely distressing. And embarrassing.

"I don't think you should read anymore." Jackson stood up, narrowly missing the lantern, and turned to leave.

"But don't you want to know your future?" Eleissa whispered to him.

Jackson stopped. He looked back at Eleissa, her knowing blue eyes looking into his. He sat back down slowly, rustling the orange sleeping bag.

"How could you possibly know the future?" he asked, thinking about the mirrors.

Eleissa opened the book to the middle, its thick pages rustling softly.

She cleared her throat. "Jackson sits back down on the orange, comfy sleeping bag and watches Eleissa doubtfully." She arched her right eyebrow. "Oh you doubt me, do you?"

Jackson shrugged uncomfortably.

"Jackson shrugs uncomfortably," she read aloud.

Jackson just watched her.

"Jackson just watches her. The Author picks up his latte and takes a sip."

Jackson shook his head. "Wait, what did you say?"

Eleissa looked back down at the book. "The Author picked up his latte and took a sip."

"What Author? Wait a minute. Who's the Author? And why did you say that 'the Author *takes* a drink,' and then when you read it again, you said he already did it. Now, I'm not a grammatical genius, but even I know when something is happening, and when something has already happened."

Eleissa smiled. "You mean the difference between the present and the not-so-distant past?"

"What Author? Who are you talking about?"

Eleissa put the book down and took a deep breath.

"Jackson, I'm going to explain something to you and I'm only going to explain it once. I'm tired of explaining it to every single person who Meeka brings in here, *unauthorized*!"

Meeka's fingers flew into her mouth. She giggled around them.

Eleissa leaned forward.

"Jackson, who do you think made you? Who do you think knows everything about you? Who do you think knows what's going to happen to you?"

Jackson shrugged his shoulders. He could think of a couple of answers, but none of them really made sense. Eleissa looked down at the book.

"You really have no idea?" she asked.

"Stop that!"

Eleissa smiled and closed the book. She leaned toward Jackson. Jackson leaned forward to her. Their noses almost touched.

"The Author," she said softly.

"The Author?" Jackson asked.

"The Author," whispered Meeka.

Eleissa's face glowed. "Jackson, you weren't made by chance. You aren't something that happened when a couple of cells merged and duplicated. You were created

by the Author, on purpose and for a purpose. Everyone
and everything was created by the Author. The Author
has written a story for everyone, and he knows how it
turns out. If you listen carefully enough, you can hear
your story. Of course no one listens anymore. No one
has time to listen to stories. They're too busy trying to
be, but they have no idea who they are *supposed* to be."

"Hang on. You're telling me that I'm created by the
Author."

Eleissa nodded.

"And that the Author created everyone."

"Yes."

"So this Author, this *great* Author who wrote my
story, this Author wrote that I would be terrible at
baseball? That I would fail in school? That I wouldn't
have any ..." he broke off, trying not to cry.

"Friends?" asked Eleissa in a quiet voice.

Jackson quickly rubbed his eyes. Meeka put her
hand on Jackson's shoulder and patted him.

"I'm your friend, Jackson."

Jackson pushed her hand off.

"Oh yeah, perfect! That's what I need! My only friend
is a make-believe little elf who lives in my great-aunt's
hair!"

Meeka shrank back as if she'd been slapped. Eleissa's eyes flashed angrily.

"You think we're make-believe?" she hissed. Meeka started to cry.

Eleissa sat back, her face hidden in the shadows. "Jackson, I can't make you believe anything. That's not my job. My job is to tell you your story, to tell you about the Author who is writing about you and that's it. If you make friends, whether you think they're make-believe or not, that's up to you. I'm just a Reader. You believe what you want."

Meeka's little sobs got a lot louder. Jackson was ashamed. He turned to Meeka.

"I'm sorry, Meeka. I'm so sorry. I didn't mean to hurt your feelings."

"I ... thought ... you ... were ... my ... my ... friend!" she gasped in between sobs.

Jackson reached out, pulled her little body over and hugged her. "I *am* your friend, Meeka. I'm so sorry. I've ... I've never had a friend before so I ... look, you *are* my friend. I'm sorry."

Meeka ran her arm across her nose, leaving a little trail of wet snot across her face.

"So I'm your first friend?" she snorted.

"Yeah, you're my first friend," replied Jackson.

"So, I'm also your best friend?"

"Yeah, I guess you are my best friend." He reached into his satchel and pulled out a tissue. He handed it to Meeka. She snorted, honking into the tissue. She hugged Jackson tightly.

"Best friend! Best friend!" she sang.

"You know, technically she's also your worst friend," said Eleissa.

Jackson glared at her. Meeka hugged Jackson tighter.

"I don't care!" she cried out.

After a few moments of hugging and "I'm sorrys," which are actually quite boring to read about, so we'll just skip them, they got back to business. Meeka snuggled very closely to Jackson. This would normally make him uncomfortable, but given that he had just hurt her feelings, he put up with it.

"So, tell me more about this Author."

"Well," Eleissa began, "He's beautiful and smart, of course, and he's very funny. He spends a lot of time writing, and everything he writes happens."

Jackson thought for a moment. "Then why did he let those ... unhappy things happen to me? To anyone, for that matter?"

Eleissa leaned in close to Jackson. "That's not for us to know."

"What?"

"The Author knows better than we do. I mean, he *did* create us after all. Jackson, the Author really cares about every single character he writes about, whether they are good or bad. The Author cares whether you eat bean burgers instead of greasy ones," she explained.

Jackson's face turned red.

"The Author knows everything. The Author plans out every single detail in your life. Everyone has a purpose because of the Author. You, me, the butterfly ... we all have a purpose."

Jackson's head spun. Eleissa turned back to the book.

"You'll get it in a minute," she said.

Jackson leaned back, lying down on the sleeping bag. Meeka handed him a purple velvet cushion edged

in gold trim, which he thanked her for and tucked comfortably under his head. His eyes focused on the swaying lantern.

And then Jackson had a good think.

I can't tell you how long he thought because time seems to fly or alternatively stop when you have a good think, and seeing as how Jackson wasn't timing himself, I have no idea. And it's completely irrelevant. What is relevant is that he took the time to think and some things need time to be thought about. So if you have something worth thinking about, I strongly suggest you get thinking on your own big think. I am delighted to tell you that he got it. But I can't tell you how Jackson got it. I can't even tell you what he was thinking about when he came to the point of getting it. But he got it. And it made sense. One day when you have the time and you can think about it, you'll get it too.

"Oh, I get it now!" Jackson exclaimed, sitting up. Meeka clapped her hands joyfully and handed him her snotty tissue. Ech. Jackson took it delicately and placed it on the floor. He turned to Eleissa.

"So can you tell me what the Author is doing now?"

Eleissa flipped the page. "The Author changes the tracks of his funky jazz music, puts his red glasses on, and asks for another latte."

Jackson grinned. He didn't get it. But he got it.

"So, now that you've started to understand the Author, is there anything else you want to know?" Eleissa asked.

Jackson thought for a moment. Eleissa glanced down at the book.

"No, don't ask me that," she said.

"Stop that!" Then he thought some more.

"The mirrors in the hall," he started. "I saw me, but I was ... older and smarter and better and stronger ..."

Eleissa nodded.

"... but how do I get there?" he finished.

Eleissa delicately fingered the book pages, not looking at him. "Jackson, I can't answer that for you."

"What do you mean? Of course you can! Just read ahead, or give me the book and I'll read it!" and he held out his hand to take the book.

Eleissa shook her head, her bangs falling into her eyes. Her nose twitched at him.

"I can't let you read it," she said slowly.

"What? Why not?"

"Because I'm the Reader. It's my job to read, and you aren't allowed to read it," she explained, shrugging her shoulders.

Jackson snatched the book from her hands and opened it.

It was blank.

"That's not fair!" he yelled, throwing the book down. It hit the floor with a heavy thud.

Eleissa nodded austerely. (*Austerely* is without humor. Like when you've just dumped your glass of milk on the dog's head, and your mother catches you and gives you *that look*.) "Life is not fair. But that's the way it goes. You aren't supposed to read your own future. If you did, you would be horrified and excited and glad and angry and sad all at the same time." She carefully picked up the book, smoothing the creased edges.

Jackson threw himself down on the sleeping bag with a huff. He was angry. But he was also very tired. No one said anything for a long time. Eleissa even stopped reading. They just sat there quietly.

After some time, Jackson sat up. "Can you at least tell me if what I saw in the mirrors is true?"

Eleissa looked fixedly at Jackson, wrapping her blonde hair around a small finger. "What you see is who you are. If you don't see that, then you're not who you are anymore."

"What are you talking about?" he asked, exasperated.

"What did you see in the mirrors?"

"Well, I was captain of the baseball team. I was a professor at the University. I won the Thompson Award."

"Did you like what you saw?"

"Well, of course I did! That's who I want to be! Those are ..." Jackson gulped. "Those are my dreams," he whispered.

"Jackson, who's to say that's not who you are now?"

"But ..."

Who indeed was to say that wasn't who he was? Just because the kids at school called him names didn't mean they were true. He was a terrible ball player, but he loved to play. And the mirror showed him as captain of the team! Those mirrors ...

The teachers called him a daydreamer, but in the picture he was a professor. He won a prize for *his* writing! How much of a daydreamer could he be if he accomplished those things? Maybe that was just for now. And if that was just for now, then it didn't matter what anyone else said. What he saw was true. Wasn't it?

"So, what I saw in the mirrors, that was true?" he asked.

"Unless you see yourself differently from the truth," she said softly. "Unless you forget."

Jackson hugged his satchel tightly and thought of the Book inside. He'd never forget. The Book would remind him if he forgot.

A beep sounded, and Eleissa flicked a button on her watch.

"Time's up. Good-bye."

Meeka stood up. "We have to go now, Jackson," she said tugging at his hand.

"But I have more questions!" he said, not moving.

"I'm very busy; please don't bother me," Eleissa sighed impatiently at them.

Jackson got up reluctantly and walked toward the open tent flap that Meeka was holding for him.

"Eleissa?"

"What?"

"Could you please stop reading my story?"

Eleissa nodded and then smiled at him.

Jackson slipped out of the tent, Meeka quietly following.

A Chapter that Is Not Nearly as Long as the Last One

In the back of your mind is a little nag nagging you. I'm not talking about an old horse nag, I'm talking about a worry, a torment, an "irk," if you will. You are probably wondering what that nag (worry, torment, irk) is. You are wondering about the doorknob on the floor in the middle of the hall. I know your mind has been going back to that doorknob and that you probably have some questions. Such as:

Why was it on the floor? Why was it not on a door? Is there a door in the floor? What is behind the door if it is indeed a door in the floor? Why on earth did Jackson forget about it? I surely didn't forget about it. Is the writer of this book having fun with me? Or is it just a pointless thing in a pointless story that is quite pointless? And when-oh-when is this book going to end? Am I going to be able to stay awake in school tomorrow with all of this reading I'm doing? Are my parents going to catch me reading in bed? Will my

mother make me go outside and play instead of finishing this book? What is with that doorknob? What is the cosine of 7.88? What is Spanish for "couch?" Why is the writer still asking all these questions? When will the writer go on?

Well, dear reader, I have some answers for you:

Because. Because. Yes. I'm getting to that. He didn't. A little. No. Soon. Doubtful. I hope not. She might. I'm getting to that. I don't know. Look it up in a Spanish-English dictionary. Because I can. Now.

chapter

39

I Bet You Thought I Forgot

Jackson and Meeka walked out the back door of the house (because the gargantuan, hairy-backed spiders were still lurking on the front porch), walked out the lovely doors painted a vivacious red, and continued with the tour.

Their walk back wasn't worth mentioning as it was rather boring in comparison to the rest of their adventure. Except when Meeka tripped on the path and the pretty weeds that smell like fishy dog breath rubbed their fishy dog breath smell on her hands. Then she

had to dig around her big bulging tour-guide bag for antibacterial wipes. ("They have those in here?" Jackson asked, to which Meeka replied, "Of course! Don't you think we care about hygiene?")

They rounded the corner of the hallway. A shiny something-or-other caught Jackson's eye, and as they approached he realized that it was the doorknob.

The doorknob.

The doorknob in the middle of the floor.

Jackson had been wondering about the doorknob but because of his adventures, he figured they would get to it eventually. As I may share with you, dear readers, that when he wanted to, Jackson could be a very patient young man. Rather unlike impatient readers.

And indeed, there the doorknob was.

chapter 40

In Which There Is a Secret

Jackson looked resolutely at the doorknob. (*Resolutely* means with determination. Like when your dog sits begging at the table and is pretty sure you'll give him a bite.) Time for a new adventure. Jackson felt unexpectedly brave. Almost like a hero would. But he had questions, of course.

"Meeka? What's up with this doorknob? Where does it go? Is there a door on the ground? What's behind the door?" Jackson asked. (I told you he had been thinking of it.)

"I really don't know," she mumbled at the floor.

"What do you mean, you don't know?"

"Um, I just don't know." She looked up at the ceiling.

Jackson stepped closer to her. "Are you not telling me something?"

Meeka jammed a fistful of hair into her mouth.

Jackson placed a hand on her shoulder. Her big brown eyes looked up at Jackson fretfully. (*Fretful* means worried. Like when your begging dog begins to whine because he's worried you won't give him a bite. Actually, that's just bad manners.)

"Meeka, do you know where this door goes?" Jackson asked.

She shook her head no, some hair falling out of her mouth.

"If you know where this door goes, why won't you tell me?"

Meeka looked up at Jackson and opened her mouth. The rest of her gacky-wet hair fell onto her shoulders. She snapped her mouth shut.

"Listen, I'm not moving anywhere until you tell me where this door goes."

Meeka looked over her shoulder, then up at the ceiling. She looked over Jackson's shoulder, then bent over and looked upside down through her legs. Then she stood up and stepped toward Jackson, putting her little mouth near his ear.

"I'm not supposed to talk about it. You're supposed to discover it for yourself," she whispered. She jerked back into position and stared at her fingernails.

This was getting altogether too complicated.

"So if I discover this doorknob by myself and open it, will you come in with me?"

Meeka looked upside down through her legs again. Jackson bent upside down and looked through his. He saw an upside-down hallway. He straightened up.

"Only because you're my friend," she whispered.

Jackson nodded at her. He pointed at the doorknob.

"Oh my!" he said in a very loud voice. "I've found a DOORKNOB! On the FLOOR, no less! I wonder where it GOES? Meeka, can I open this door?"

"SURE YOU CAN!"

Jackson kneeled down. He turned the doorknob and...

In Which the Writer
Prepares You

I want to prepare you for this part. You aren't going to like it. You aren't going to like it at all. And it's going to frustrate you. But then you'll like it again. That's all I can really tell you right now. So you'd better keep reading.

... and ...

chapter

42

A Chapter that Requires
a Key Again

... it was locked.

"Oh, for *crying out loud*!!!" Jackson yelled.

Meeka squeaked and jumped back.

"Why won't this door open?" He turned to her.

Meeka squeaked again. She trembled and muttered something.

"What?"

"It's locked."

"I can see that it's locked, Meeka," Jackson said superciliously. (*Supercilious* means arrogant and grouchy. I've already explained it back on page 133. Don't you remember?)

Meeka's head hung lower.

Oh, for crying out loud!

"I'm sorry, Meeka. Yes, it is locked. Would you happen to have the key?"

Meeka trembled. "I'm going to get fired."

"Why are you going to get fired?"

"I lost the key. Again."

"Where did you lose the key, Meeka?"

"I don't know," she wailed, throwing her little arms into the air. "It's the same key that opens the gate of the house. And the trapdoor! And this door! And I LOST IT!"

"What trapdoor?"

"Er ... never mind." Meeka's fingers twisted her hair.

"Well, isn't there a spare key we can use?"

"I've lost it! And the other, *other* spare is at the house. BUT I LOST THAT TOO!" Meeka threw herself against the wall and pounded it with her fists. "I'm going to get fired! I always lose things! WHAAAAAA!"

Jackson was annoyed, but he didn't want to upset Meeka further. Nothing is worse than a screaming girl. Except maybe a crying girl. And she was doing both. No point exacerbating the situation. (*Exacerbating* is like when you pick your scab and then it bleeds more,

156

and your mother tells you to stop doing that because
you'll just make it worse.)

Jackson sat down against the wall and contemplated
the doorknob. Meeka slid from the wall to the floor and
just sat there, her little hands covering her big eyes.
Every once in a while she'd sniffle. Then snort. Jackson
needed to take charge of the situation.

"Meeka, you were the one who unlocked the gate. Do
you remember what you did with the key?" he asked.

Meeka shook her head.

"Okay, let's backtrack a little. What happened after
you unlocked the gate? You followed Rayaa to chase
the crubbie right?"

Meeka nodded, her fingers going into her mouth.

"Okay, Rayaa shot the crubbie, and then what
happened?" he asked.

"Mmmmphaaamphhhaaaoooomphhhsssssssmphhh."

"What did you say?"

Meeka removed her hands from her mouth. "I went
to look at the birdcage."

"Okay, and then what?"

"Then I climbed up on the perch. I was thinking
about cat food."

"Sorry?"

"Cat food. How gross it is.
I was imaging how gross cat
food tastes."

"You've tasted cat food?"
Jackson scratched his head.

"And I remembered it so
vividly that I had a yucky
taste in my mouth, so I
wanted a piece of gum."

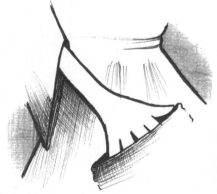

"So what did you do with the
key?"

Meeka's eyes popped with delight. She
slid her hand into her left pocket and ...

In Which the Story Continues

Well of *course* the key was there. Why else would there be such a buildup? I mean, did you think Jackson would walk away from the doorknob? That's just silly. Of course he was going to unlock the door. If he didn't, the story would no longer be interesting and you would write me many letters to state your disappointment. I might get UN-fan mail. And that just wouldn't do. I'm all for encouraging letters, but I don't need letters on how I am a bad writer, how I drink too many chai lattes, or that it's silly to shriek when one encounters earwigs. Er ... never mind.

By the way, the disappointment is coming.

Just to warn you.

Meeka slid her hand in her left pocket and pulled out a key.

"Good girl, Meeka!" Jackson shouted.

She beamed a big smile from elf ear to elf ear.

Jackson took the key from her, slipped it into the lock, and turned it and ...

chapter

44

A Chapter that Is
Terribly Mean

... I'm so mean ...

chapter 45

A Chapter that Is Even More Mean

. . . it turned . . .

In Which No One Can
Find a Light Switch

Jackson took a big breath and pulled. The floor opened as the door swung open. Jackson looked into the hole. Well, he tried to. It was dark. Very dark. Actually, it was pitch-black. Jackson looked back at Meeka.

"Meeka, is there a light switch or something?"

Meeka shook her head and said nothing. She slunk backward to the wall and sat down. Jackson sighed and looked back down the hole.

"Hello!" he called out. His voice was swallowed by the darkness.

A light came on, blinding Jackson.

"Hello."

A Chapter that Explains a Lot

Could I be meaner? Actually, yes I could. I could totally change the subject of this chapter and drive you absolutely bananas and make you want to throw this book against the wall in frustration or even write an UN-fan letter. Now it is really making you crazy with wanting to know what is behind that door. Well, I'm done toying with your emotions, and I will let the story continue on. This is a long chapter so make sure you take the time to read it, because when you begin you will not want to stop.

Jackson rubbed his eyes. A head popped out from the bright light. The head had short, spiky, blond hair and kind eyes. He smiled a big smile, his teeth twinkling because he had braces.

"They have braces in here?" Jackson wondered aloud.

This was a rather rude thing to say. Jackson should have said, "Hello, how do you do?" which are the appropriate words to say after someone says hello (unless of course it's a stranger down a dark alley, in which case you should run the other way). But you must understand that Jackson had seen so many strange things that day, he was a little surprised to see something so normal. Oh sorry, I'm keeping you from the story. My bad.

The head laughed a deep laugh.

"Yes, we have braces in here. I wear them because my teeth are crooked."

Jackson just stared at him.

"You coming in?" he asked.

Jackson looked down.

"Oh, it's all right," the man said, seeming to read his mind. "There are stairs leading down, but they're steep, so watch your step."

He stepped down and Jackson took a step to follow him. He looked back at Meeka who was sitting against the wall.

"Are you coming?" He was a little nervous, and he wanted her to come with him.

Meeka paused and then stepped forward. "Just don't tell anyone I came with you and Josh. I'm really not supposed to."

"Oh, his name is Josh?"

Meeka nodded. "Josh the Page."

"Josh the page?"

"No, not like a page in a book. A page is like, well ..." And she trailed off.

Josh's voice drifted up from the stairs below. "A page is a messenger and an apprentice."

But Jackson hadn't heard him. Well, he had heard him, but once Jackson saw where the stairs led, he

stopped listening. And the reason he stopped listening was because ...

The stairs led into a large forest.

Jackson stepped down the last step onto the forest floor. The ground was springy under his feet. Soft moss grew everywhere. This was the most beautiful forest Jackson had ever seen. And he had seen his fair share of forests, especially for a ten-and-a-half-year-old.

Gigantic trees filled the sky. Their colossal limbs flared out, reaching for the bright sun. Massive black oaks (*Quercus velutina*), spreading silver maples (*Acer saccharinum*), and dominant yellow birches (*Betula alleghaniensis*). (I've included the Latin names in case you are of a scientific mind.)

The forest also had glittering silver poplars (*Populus alba*), golden weeping willows (*Salix alba* var. *vitellina*), gothic jack pine (*Pinus banksiana*), and silvery Russian olives (*Eleagnus angustifolia*). (I'm sure you are asking yourself what Russian olive trees are doing in such a forest, as they are an ornamental tree. I would ask the same question but it is one of my favorite trees, so I don't particularly mind.)

A dried-up mud path led away from the stairs. The
kind of dry mud path that makes lovely slap-slap
noises when you walk on it barefoot. Meeka confessed
that she'd spent last Saturday doing just that and not
much else.

Jackson blinked and turned to look at Josh the
Page.

Josh the Page was younger than Jackson had pre-
viously thought. He was about eighteen, and he had
curious green eyes and wore a gold hoop in his left
ear. His green short-sleeved uniform shirt showed off
strong arms. His shirt was tucked into his green hiking shorts. He had solid hiking boots on with very tight
laces. He had a brown belted leather satchel slung over
one shoulder. And he had a twinkle smile that one can
only achieve if they wear twinkly braces.

Jackson had a million questions.

"I have a million questions," Jackson said.

"Go ahead."

But what Jackson asked was unexpected. He didn't ask why there was a forest below the stairs. He didn't ask how a forest could possibly exist in a room. He didn't even ask who had planted the ornamental Russian olive trees, because they clearly did not belong in such a place. What he did ask was:

"What are you apprenticing for?"

Josh the Page laughed. Meeka laughed as well. Jackson just looked at the two of them and felt a little unsettled. They just kept laughing. He waited patiently. They kept laughing.

Josh wiped the tears from his eyes.

"Oh, that was a good one. You could have asked me what a forest was doing below the stairs, or how it could possibly exist in this room. You didn't even ask who planted the ornamental Russian olive trees, because they clearly do not belong in such a place as this. Instead you go directly to the most unobvious question to ask. This is why you were chosen for the tour."

Meeka chewed on the ends of her hair.

"Jackson, I'm apprenticing to be a Dreamgiver," he said.

Jackson nodded, as if to say, "Please go on as I need more information, and you'd better use words I understand because I don't feel like standing around all day asking questions about answers that I need to keep asking questions about in order to get the answer." You know that nod. I'm sure you've given it yourself.

171

"Let's walk." They turned down the path. "I assume you've heard all about the Author from Eleissa? Knowing Meeka, she took you to see Eleissa. She can't help but show off her family."

Meeka twittered behind them and Josh smiled at her. Jackson stopped walking.

They had come to a river.

The river was calm as the water slowly trickled by. It looked cool and refreshing. It was the kind of river that made you desperately thirsty just looking at it. Weeping willows stretched their long branches over the water, their tips dangling like lazy fingers, drawing enigmatic circles in its current. You could imagine yourself leaning against those glorious willows, their long branches hiding you in your own private shady oasis. You could lay there for hours, throwing duck feed at ducks, twiddling cattails in your fingers and daydreaming about absolutely nothing. Jackson could hear the calls of the birds hidden in the limbs. A chirping frog called its mate.

"The Author created every one of us, which makes us the same. No one is more important than another, or less important. We are all equal. The thing that separates everyone, that makes each person special, is the story he created for each of us. And each story is full of excitement and adventure, sadness and joy. And each story, your story, my story, Meeka's story—they all intertwine, like rope."

"Or like hair?" Jackson mused aloud.

Josh laughed. "Yeah, like hair."

Josh bent down and picked up a pine needle. He twirled it gently between his fingers as he kept talking. "But people have a choice. They can be the hero in their own story and succeed, or they can try to be the hero in someone else's story and fail."

"What do you mean?"

Josh's serene voice continued. "Let's say someone was born to play the piano. His purpose, the story of his life, was to make beautiful music. And the people who listened to his music, they would have felt his happiness, the joy that comes from doing what the Author wanted him to do. But let's say this same man decided to listen to what the world told him. And in this case, the world told him to be a successful businessman. So he worked very hard at learning the numbers and the ways of business. But as he got older, he strayed further and further away from his story, and soon he forgot he had one. He was secretly unhappy and had no idea why. But it was because it wasn't his story he was living out; it was someone else's. His story was to become a pianist. It was ingrained into his soul by the Author, and he chose to ignore that desire."

Jackson thought very hard about this. Josh smiled and continued. "My job, as an apprentice," he said, "is to help people remember that they have a story." The pine needle in Josh's hand twirled faster. He looked at Jackson. "That's my story." Josh looked intently at the pine needle in his fingers. "I have the same story my mom did," Josh murmured.

"Where's your mom now?"

"She's doing her own job of helping people." Josh paused, staring at the river. "Ever since I was little boy, I've wanted to do what she does. She's on the other side, so I haven't seen her in a very long time." He cleared his throat and smiled lightly at Jackson. "So now I'm apprenticing, learning how to be a part of the Dreamgivers. It's not easy, and there's a lot of studying, but it's worth every second."

Jackson watched the trees sway gently, and he thought about what Josh said.

He thought about how he always wanted to be a writer. He had millions of story ideas, and it was just a matter of time before he wrote them all out. He knew they were good ideas, and of course they needed a lot

of work. But he was only ten and a half, for goodness' sakes. He thought about how he wanted to play ball professionally. To feel the hot sun on his head as he squinted at the catcher, the tension on the field as he prepared for the windup, the snap as he let go of that perfect pitch, and the screaming fans.

Jackson's chest tightened. He felt like crying. Not because he was sad, but because, well, his heart was full. You know that feeling when you're reflecting on your own story and your heart wants to just burst out of your chest because you are filled with so much hope?

Jackson wiped his eyes quickly. "So how do you help people remember their stories?"

"I lead them to the path. And then I let them lead themselves."

"What do you mean?"

Josh the Page eyed Jackson. "Are you ready to go on your own?"

"Um, uh, I don't know," he stuttered.

Josh the Page nodded. "Then come with me."

Jackson followed him down to the river's edge, with Meeka trailing quietly behind them. The rays of sunlight misted through the branches of the trees. The river's gurgling became louder. They stopped and listened for a moment.

"Jackson. Do you know who you are?" Josh the Page asked.

"Well, I know who my parents are."

"No. Who *you* are. What makes up Jackson?"

Jackson thought for a moment. "Well, I like playing baseball, even though I'm not very good." He glanced away, embarrassed. "I think I'm pretty smart, even though I can't understand algebra. I think my stories are good, even though my grammar is atrocious. And I think I'd make a pretty good friend."

Meeka nodded enthusiastically at him.

"And the Author made me, so he must have some purpose for me, in his story, right?" Jackson's voice caught in his throat.

"You need to remember that," said Josh the Page. "You need to hold onto those truths very tightly."

"Why?"

Josh pointed at the water. "You'll find a lot of stones in this river, and you have to choose one. It might be hard to find, but if you remember the Author and what he's doing for you, you'll find the right one. It will be a stone that's calling your name."

Jackson gazed at the river. The river was narrow, with long grasses and willow branches grazing the embankments. It went on, curving gracefully to the left. It was so peaceful that Jackson wanted very much to walk down that stream, to feel the cool water tickle his toes, with the branches shading him from the sun.

Jackson looked at Josh, and Josh smiled, but his eyes were very serious. Meeka looked down at her boots.

Jackson began to feel the seriousness of the situation. This wasn't just a walk down the river. No siree, this was—dare I say it?—a quest. A very important, life-altering quest.

I just want to interrupt for a moment here before you get right into the story.

In your life there will be many quests, some as mundane as picking out your socks and some as exciting as picking out your socks. It all depends on how you feel about socks. Very few quests in your life will be important and life-altering. However, the important and life-altering quests are of a most serious nature. And when they come, you need to consider them very carefully, because they are indeed life-altering. I can't tell you how, because I am not you.

Jackson's hands sweated. He wiped them on his pants, leaving wet handprints. His upper lip was wet. He wiped it on his sleeve, leaving a wet trail. He felt like he was about to do a pop quiz.

"So I just step into the river?" Jackson asked.

"Yes."

"And I just have to find my stone?"

"Yes."

"And then I come back?"

"Yes."

"And that's all I have to do?"

Josh's green eyes held Jackson's. He said nothing.

Jackson breathed deeply and looked at the water. Bits of leaves and twigs floated downstream. He placed his foot into the water. It was cool, but not very cold. In

fact, it was rather refreshing. His red pajamas clung wetly to his legs. Annoying, but bearable.

Jackson looked up at Josh, who sat down on the riverbank. Meeka stood beside him. They both smiled.

Jackson readjusted his satchel and took another step. And then another. And another.

In Which the Quest Begins

The water trickled, gurgling and rushing against larger rocks. Jackson peered at the sandy bottom of the river. Tiny little minnows swam away from his moving feet, creating little clouds of fine sand in their wake. Jackson stepped carefully down the river, searching for stones. He bent down, his fingertips reaching into the cool, clear water. They scratched the bottom, and he pulled up a handful of sand. There were little bits of shell crushed by time in the sand, but no stones. He threw the wet sand, listening to the "plops" as it hit the water. He kept walking, but his focus was interrupted by the beauty overhead. The sun dazzled him, poking her head out between the giant boughs of the willows lining the bank. He stopped and smiled into the sky. If only he could bring a piece of this home with him! Jackson shook himself and kept walking. Stop daydreaming.

A black stone twinkled at him in the water. He bent down and picked it up.

A Chapter that Involves
More Questing

The black stone was smooth and fit snuggly into Jackson's hand. Words were etched into it. Jackson squinted to read.

You have ugly hair.

Jackson laughed out loud. Okay, *that* was silly. That definitely couldn't be his stone. It was too ridiculous. He skipped the stone beautifully on the water before it slipped under the surface. Jackson smiled to himself. His throwing was getting better!

He shifted his satchel. It was a little uncomfortable. Keep moving.

Jackson's eyes caught on another rock, so he picked it up.

You play baseball atrociously.

What a ridiculous thing to write on a stone! Jackson laughed, but it was a hollow laugh. He swallowed, a little self-conscious. What a strange coincidence. How would a rock know if he was a good baseball player or not? Jackson knew he wasn't a *great* baseball player. But still. This couldn't be his rock. He tossed it into the water, watching uneasily as ripples bounced off the shore.

Jackson walked more slowly. He shifted his satchel, the strap digging into his shoulders. A stone winked at him from the water. He slowly picked it up. It was a dark gray with black writing.

You are stupid.

Jackson felt sick. He almost sat down in the water he felt so sick. A big lead ball had rolled into his belly, and it wasn't leaving.

"I'm not stupid! I can read and I'm a great writer and I ..." Jackson's voice faltered.

But he didn't understand algebra. He couldn't remember what all the countries' capitals were. He couldn't remember all the countries, for that matter. He didn't know the cosine of 7.88. And he definitely did not know what "couch" was in Spanish.

Jackson frowned at the stone in his hand. It was smooth, and his thumb fit right into a groove, like it was meant to. Was this his stone? It couldn't be.

Could it?

Jackson watched the stone slip from his fingers into the water. It splashed, the water soaking the front of his legs. Great. He shifted his satchel. It was cramp-

ing him in crampable places. (Yes, I know that's not a word, but it should be.)

Jackson walked slowly and pensively around the river's bend. (*Pensive* is like when you're concentrating so hard, you don't notice that your sister has dropped an ice cube down your back until it's too late.)

A Very Gloomy Chapter

Jackson surveyed the river gloomily, barely noticing the change in scenery. His head was full of
thoughts. And not many of them were pleasant. He
glanced up at the weeping willows (*Salix alba* var. *vitellina*), not noticing that their branches were less full,
less weeping, and not as trailing. He squinted into the
bright sky as beads of sweat dripped down his back.
Jackson rubbed his arm across his forehead. His wet
pajamas were beginning to scratch his legs. He walked
on, dragging his feet.

The stream was no longer refreshing. He could feel
little blisters popping up on his heels. He wanted to
take his shoes off, to feel the soft, sandy bottom, but
the soft, sandy bottom was now rocky
and slippery. He found a few
smaller stones hidden in crev-
ices, but they were just stones.

About half an hour passed
before Jackson spotted
another etched stone. He
picked it up hesitantly.

You have no friends.

Jackson's mouth felt like it
was full of cotton. He tried to

swallow but he couldn't. He laughed but the empty sky sucked away the sound.

It was true.

He didn't have any friends. Lunchtime at school meant hiding in the library. If it was nice out, he'd walk to the highway bridge and sit on the stairs, alone. He was always chosen last to play games in gym class.

Jackson's heart hurt.

He took a few more steps and his eyes blurred. He drew a ragged breath as he tried not to cry. He couldn't cry. Not here.

Jackson stood there for a long time, turning the stone over and over in his hands.

It was time to go back. But how could this be the end? This wasn't what the Author wanted for him, was it?

His satchel was getting very heavy now. Jackson readjusted the strap, but it was still uncomfortable. And he was thirsty. What if he drank from the stream? He looked down, but the water was murky. He couldn't drink that. His gaze shifted to the river's edge. The forest was no longer familiar.

Instead of lush willows there were scraggly black spruce (*Picea mariana*), their thick, dry, scrubby branches unmoving in the sun's glare. No breeze, no clouds in the sky. It was a wasteland. A bleak, deserted wasteland.

Just like his dreams.

Just like him.

Jackson sighed heavily. He studied the stone he held, unable to move. The murkiness of the river shifted and Jackson saw another etched stone. He picked it up with a little hope in his heart. It had to be better.

You are not worth loving.

Hot, heavy tears fell from Jackson's eyes. He was so tired, so sad, so lonely.

He wasn't good at anything.

He was bad at baseball.

No one cared about his stories.

He had no friends.

He was alone.

Jackson's shoulders slumped and the satchel fell off. It splashed into the water, speckling Jackson's face with mud. He didn't care. He watched the satchel float slowly away. What did it matter? It was just a bag, a bag of no importance, belonging to a boy of no importance. He wiped his face with his sleeve. Yes, of course it was gross, but what else was he going to do? He hadn't perfected the art of a snot rocket.

"Help!"

In Which a Hero Is Needed

"Help me! Please!"

Jackson jammed the stones into his pajama pockets and ran down the river. He slipped and fell. The river's thin, drippy mud soaked his face, but Jackson got up and kept running. He heard a loud gurgling and followed the sound, his blood running cold at the sight ahead.

A waterfall!

Jackson ran down the river's edge, trying desperately to keep his balance. He ducked and dodged the branches as they scratched him, pulling at his shirt and hair.

"Hello? Where are you?"

"I'm up here! I mean, down here! Just help me!" the voice squeaked.

"Meeka!"

In Which Steps Are Taken
to Become a Hero

Jackson scrambled to the riverbank, his feet slip-
ping in the shifting sand. He seized the dried prickly
shrubs and pulled himself out. He ran down the riverbank, leaping over rocks and clumps of dead branches
that were scattered about the forest floor. The dead
trees sliced his bare arms with their little stiff twigs
as he pushed through. A branch slashed his cheek
and a searing white pain burned his face. But he kept
running.

Jackson reached the edge of a cliff, his chest
pounding, his breath ragged from running. He looked
over the side.

chapter

53

A Chapter that Is a Little Scary

Meeka was stuck in a tree. A dead tree. A dead tree that was lying on its side, hanging over the edge of the cliff. Meeka clung desperately to something hanging in its brittle branches.

Jackson's satchel!

Meeka's long hair plastered her wet face, her little body soaked from the waterfall splashing ten feet away from her. Her big eyes bore into Jackson, who stared at her in disbelief and shock.

"Jackson! Help me, please!" she screamed.

Jackson snapped, "Meeka! Don't move!"

She cried, her sobs barely heard over the pounding and splashing of the waterfall.

"Don't cry! Be brave! Just hold on tight!" Jackson scrambled down the side of the cliff, and then his feet slipped and he landed hard on his back. He scrambled up quickly, ignoring the pain in his shoulder blades. He stepped carefully, holding onto the dead branches of the fallen tree, making sure every step held while he walked the precarious trunk. (*Precarious* in this case means the tree might break at any moment, so why are you even walking on it?)

He couldn't go any farther. There was nothing left to hold onto. And the tip of the tree wouldn't hold him.

Meeka's eyes were shut tight, and her face was white with shock. Her little fingers clutched the satchel as it held by one slowly ripping strap.

"Everything is okay, Meeka. I'm here. Just don't let go!" Jackson yelled over the rushing waterfall.

"Okay," squeaked her little voice. It was a long drop, the water churning and bubbling at the bottom, waiting to eat whatever fell off the edge. Sharp, menacing rocks poked out of the water.

Oh, dear.

Jackson stretched himself out on the trunk, trying to reach Meeka. She was too far away. He tried to think of stories where he had seen this kind of thing before. He didn't have any rope. There weren't any extra branches for her to grab.

He couldn't reach her. He couldn't reach the bag. He crept along the trunk. The tree began to bend into the ravine.

The branch tore. It sounded exactly like the cracking of knucklebones.

Jackson's heart sank in desperation. There was nothing he could do. Absolutely nothing. The pounding in his heart matched the pain in his head. *I can't do anything. I can't save her,* raced through his mind.

Jackson eased backward off the trunk, shuffling along until he could stand up. He searched frantically for a branch or something he could hold out to Meeka. Nothing. He checked his pockets, looking for something, anything that would help; a rope, a trampoline, an idea, something. He pulled out two stones. *You have no friends,* read one. *You are not worth loving,* read the other.

A fiery anger burned within him. *Meeka is my friend.* Jackson chucked the stones to the ground. He thought of the Author who created him, the Author who gave him his dreams, his life, his hardships, his struggles. Who gave him a friend.

"NO!" Jackson yelled. His mind spun furiously.

It came to him. He knew what he had to do.

He had to save Meeka's life.

Even if ... even if ...

Jackson didn't think the rest of the sentence. Instead, he thought about the Author. He thought about the Author writing his story. He thought about being the hero. And he knew what he had to do. Jackson looked at the fallen tree, and then looked at Meeka.

He ran as fast as he could.

And jumped.

chapter 54

In Which a Hero Is Born

Jackson soared through the air, and his hands flayed until he snagged the branch. He swung himself up and hugged Meeka's sobbing body.

"I've got you."

"I know," she whimpered.

The branch broke.

In Which We Wait for Death

The air rushed around their falling bodies. Jackson shut his eyes tightly, holding Meeka closer. He heard the sounds of the churning water beneath them. Jackson turned, holding Meeka on top of him.

So he would hit the rocks first.

She will not die, she will not die, she will not die. Jackson's thoughts repeated. *But why isn't my life flashing before my eyes? I wonder if there's a heaven. Is my hamster there? What about my grandma? I should have hugged Mom. I hope she's not too sad that I'm gone.*

There were other thoughts that I will not divulge, because some things are just too personal. And it's none of your business.

Meeka squeezed Jackson, her chin on his shoulder, her legs wrapped around his waist. He held her tighter. He waited for the crash.

In Which We Meet
Another Hero

A hoy!" a voice called out.
"Jackson, look!"

Jackson's eyes popped open. They weren't falling. They weren't even moving. He looked around and
realized that they were hanging in midair. The satchel
strap had snagged a tree. A different tree.

Am I kidding you?

No. I am not.

"Want some help?"

Jackson turned his head to look behind him.

Josh!

chapter 57

In Which No One Dies

Josh stood on a ledge three feet from them. His arms
stretched out to Meeka, and Jackson loosened his
grip on her. She planted her feet on Jackson's thighs
and jumped to Josh's arms. He hugged her and put
her down. Jackson stretched out a trembling hand and
Josh grabbed it tightly.

Jackson looked at Josh.
Josh's face was calm and he
was smiling.

"Trust me," he said softly.

Jackson swallowed.

One ... two ... three.

Josh yanked him, hard.

Jackson couldn't stand on his
wobbly legs. Josh held him upright.

"Thank you," Jackson stammered. His
heart beat wildly in his chest.

"Have you found your stone yet?" Josh asked.

"Um ... maybe? I thought I had, but ..." he trailed
off.

Josh nodded.

"I'll see you at the finish line," he said. And he left,
climbing effortlessly up the cliff.

You'd think there would be more conversation here.
That Josh would stay and answer the many questions

that Jackson might have. But when you face death, death that you know is coming whether you like it or not, and then it doesn't happen, you don't talk much. So Jackson really had nothing to say. His mind was void of questions. All he could think was ...

Meeka didn't die.

chapter 58

In Which There Is a Great Deal of Dancing

Jackson staggered down the path alongside the cliff and climbed to the bottom when ...

"Gaagh! Ger off!" he gagged.

Meeka loosened her grip a little from his neck.

"Oh, Jackson! Thank you! You saved my life!" she squeaked as she danced around.

Jackson shook her off, trying to regain his balance. "Meeka ... MEEKA! What were you doing up on that cliff?"

Meeka stopped dancing, her hair wild in her face. "Well, you dropped your satchel, and I thought you might miss it, so I went after it."

"You were following me?" Jackson asked incredulously.

Meeka shrugged, casually pushing the hair off her face.

"I almost *died! You* almost died! Are you *crazy?*" he yelled.

"But I didn't! And you didn't! So it's okay!" And she danced again.

Jackson looked at her in disbelief. "But you could have!"

"But I didn't!" Meeka twirled even faster.

She spun right into a tree. She fell down, laughing. Jackson looked back at the waterfall, blinking in amazement and confusion. Its menacing churning splashes waved at him. Not literally, of course. Water can't wave at you; it just has waves. Oh, never mind.

Meeka grabbed Jackson's hands and twirled him.

"Meeka, STOP it!" Jackson shouted and he yanked his hands from hers. Meeka looked at Jackson, surprised, and then she twirled off.

Jackson picked up his soggy bag from the ground. It was ruined. The strap was ripped. It was very, very heavy. He opened it and turned it upside down to empty it. The contents fell to the ground with a big splash.

There was the Book.

Jackson paused for a moment and then picked up the Book. The pages were thick with water. He peeled open the first page. The writing was smudged.

It was ruined.

He carefully peeled back another page.

Smudged.

Next page?

Smudged as well.

Next page?

You guessed it.

Jackson sighed bitterly. He dropped to the ground, leaning uncomfortably against a dead spruce. He looked around dispassionately. (*Dispassion* is when you have no passion. Like when your mom tells you you're having leftovers ... again. What's your emotion? Dispassion.)

Meeka twirled about, kicking up bits of dust in the air as she spun. And then she fell over from dizziness. She giggled a little and then just lay there quietly, looking up into the sky. She hummed something indistinct. Jackson turned another sticky-wet page in his book. He couldn't make out any of the words.

What had they said before? He couldn't remember. It didn't matter anymore. If the words were important, he would have remembered, wouldn't he? His heart felt ... empty.

He felt empty.

Jackson lay down and stared at the sky. His body was so tired. His head hurt, his chest hurt, and he was getting hot again. Jackson placed the Book over his face covering his eyes from the glare. And within a moment, he was asleep.

In Which Meeka Is Bossy

"Jackson! Jackson!"

Jackson opened his eyes to darkness. He pulled the Book off his face and squinted in the bright sun. He was groggy. And tired. He felt strangely sad. And still empty.

"Jackson, we have to finish the Tour," Meeka said worriedly.

Jackson looked at his watch. It was five in the morning. Five in the morning. He didn't care. He put the Book back over his eyes. Quiet, darkness … ah, much better.

Wait a minute! Five a.m.! Oh no! He had to get back home! He wasn't allowed to be out this late! Technically he hadn't left his room, but still! His parents would definitely notice he wasn't in bed.

Jackson sat up quickly, grunting as his shoulder blades burned with pain. "But I lost my stones."

Meeka gave him a hard look. She put her little hands on her hips and her face screwed up in anger. "Well, you'd better find them, *buster*! You might be my friend, but you will NOT be the one to keep me from being promoted! I've got dreams too you know, and they do not involve remaining a TOUR GUIDE!"

Jackson was taken aback. But he stood up resolutely and brushed the spruce needles and dust off his butt. (Of course I had to use the word *butt*, it's a funny word.) He picked up his ripped satchel and tucked it under his arm. He picked up the Book, and Meeka's little hand grabbed his. And they walked down the forest path that led away from the cliff.

In Which Jackson Hurries

Sometimes in stories time goes by in the adventure, but not at home. Like in that fabulous book about wardrobes and Turkish delight. This was not the case for Jackson. The actual minutes passing in this adventure were the exact minutes at home, in Jackson's room, in Jackson's bed. Jackson's dad would be snoring away down the hall, and his mom would occasionally yell out "Stop snoring!" And he'd hear his dad mutter something and then start snoring again. His little sister would have her thumb in her mouth and her little stuffed puppy dog under her arm. His little brother would have thrown off all the sheets and be sleeping with his mouth wide open and his arms spread out. Great-Aunt Harriett would be snoring. In two hours, the newspaper would hit the door with a thud, the dog would bark at the door, Dad would sit up and yell at the dog, and Mom would get out of bed and go downstairs to make coffee and breakfast. His little sister would climb out of her crib and come into Jackson's room to wake him up. But he wouldn't be there. Not unless he hurried. So we'd better yell at Jackson to hurry up.

HURRY UP, JACKSON!!!!!

Jackson lifted his head. He thought he heard voices yelling at him to hurry up. But it was quiet except for

211

the sound of the river. He shrugged his shoulders and kept walking, holding Meeka's warm little hand.

Jackson clambered into the river, in an eddy where it was safe. The water was stagnant and brown in this area. (*Stagnant* means not moving, in case you didn't have a dictionary handy and really, you should always have a dictionary handy to look up words you read but don't understand and not rely on people like me to explain everything.) Jackson imagined creatures lurking in the water, waiting to grab his ankles. Kind of like his mom's cabbage-brussels-sprout-beet stew. Not that anything in the stew has grabbed his ankles, but one never knows.

Meeka climbed into the river to follow him.

"No, wait," said Jackson. "I have to do this on my own."

Meeka paused a moment and then nodded. She climbed back out and stood on the riverbank.

Jackson gave her a small smile and, with a wave, walked downstream.

chapter

61

In Which No Questions Are Answered

Will this story ever end? Will Jackson find his stones? Will he give up? What is the cosine of 7.88? What is Spanish for "couch?"

Yes. Keep reading. Keep reading. Get a calculator. Get a Spanish-English dictionary.

On we go.

chapter

62

In Which a Heart Hurts

Jackson tripped.

He fell into the water, face first. Oh, it was disgusting. The water went up his nose and into his mouth because as he fell, he opened his mouth to say "Oh, I'm falling." But all that came out was "Oh" and then his mouth filled with disgusting, brown, stagnant water. He quickly sat up, choking and coughing. The water tasted awful. Imagine a lovely glass of fresh water. Then mix in some mud, some little tiny rocks, some desiccated crawfish shells, some fish poop, and some algae. That's what it tasted like. Blech.

But just as he was thinking how awful it was, Jackson felt something underneath his hand. His fingers closed around the something, and he pulled two stones up out of the water. They were engraved.

Your dreams are not real, read one.

You are not special, read the other.

Jackson didn't bother getting up. He just sat there looking at the stones, turning them over and over in his hands.

"These are my stones," he thought dully. And then he began to cry. Not like the little tears that slip out when you've hit your thumb with a hammer, and not like the selfish tears that leak out when your brother got the last piece of wedding cake with blue roses. No,

215

these were the huge tears that pop out of your eyes and
plunge to the ground, your body shaking as your nose
gets completely stuffed up, and your lips are quivering,
and all you want is to be held by your mom and have
her whisper to you, "This too shall pass."

After a few good minutes of crying, Jackson wiped
his eyes. He wiped his nose on his sleeve. (Yes, of
course it was gross, but what else was he going to do?)

He calmed down. He didn't feel any better. But now
he could go home. He had found his stones.

Jackson thought he'd be happier than this.

He looked around for Meeka. But she was nowhere
to be seen. Why would she be? He had told her he
wanted to be alone, but, at that moment, he missed
her.

The stones fit perfectly into the palms of Jackson's
hands. They were smooth and not too heavy and had
little twinkling sparkles in them. They looked like
Josh's braces.

Jackson lifted his head and watched the Book float
away. And at that moment, Jackson made a very seri-

ous, life-altering, life-changing decision. He grasped the two gray stones in his hand and, with a swift arc, threw them far down the river. *Good throw*, he thought to himself, pleased.

Jackson turned and splashed down the river, chasing after the Book. Just as it was within his reach he tripped again, but he reached out his hands and caught it before the current could take it away. He opened the cover gently, but one glance told him that the pages were more waterlogged than before. He definitely wouldn't be able to read it now.

Jackson felt very tired. He lay back in the river. The muddy water felt cool on his hot head. It trickled down the sides of his face, into his ears, and inside his pajama shirt. "Remember who you are. Who am I? The Author made me for a purpose ... yeah, right."

"Jackson."

Jackson sat up carefully.

It was quiet.

Very quiet. Not a sound to be heard at all. Not even a bird calling out.

He should get going. It was time to go back, to go back home, to go back to ... But it felt good to lie down, to do nothing. Jackson lay down again, the water tickling his face. The clouds were far away in the hot blue sky. If only he could have some shade. If only he could eat something. If only ...

"Jackson."

Jackson lay very still. He held his breath. The water was still trickling, making little rushing noises, but the voices were louder.

"Jackson."

He sat up very slowly. He looked into the water, but it was so dirty, he couldn't see anything. He ran his fingers along the bottom of the river. His fingers trailed over stones. He grabbed a handful. He opened his hand to look at them. Plain, smooth, white stones.

"Jackson."

Jackson stared at the rocks in his hand. Then he brought his hand to his ear.

"Jackson."

He picked up a single one and held it to his ear.

"Jackson," it whispered softly.

He brought the handful to his ear.

"Jackson," they called out.

Jackson picked up his ripped bag and his waterlogged Book and began walking up the river, back to Meeka and back to where Josh the Page was waiting for him.

chapter

In Which Things Are Not as They Seem

There is no point in telling you about the walk back because nothing interesting happened. Well, if you don't count Meeka climbing a tree and falling into thorn bushes. And if you don't count Meeka prying off one of Jackson's shoes and throwing it at a bird who was squawking loudly at them. And if you don't count how they got the shoe back. Those are different stories for different times, and they really don't have anything to do with this book's climax. So we'll just skip those parts and continue. If you wish to know what happened, then just send me a letter, and I'll forward you those few paragraphs. But I'll tell you right now, they are just fillers.

Jackson climbed up the riverbank. Josh the Page sat under a golden weeping willow, the branches shading him. He looked up at them and smiled.

Josh stood up and Meeka ran over, giving him a big hug. "Well?" he asked.

Jackson swallowed nervously. What if he had failed? He reached into his pockets and held out the stones for Josh to see. Josh looked down into Jackson's hand, and then laughed.

"So how was the adventure?"

"Well, if you hadn't shown up and saved us, I probably wouldn't be here."

"I came to save you?"

"Yeah, if you hadn't been there to get us out of that tree, we would have fallen."

"We almost *died!*" Meeka shouted.

Josh's smile faltered. "I never left this bank, Jackson."

"But that's impossible!" spluttered Jackson. "Meeka fell of a cliff and was holding onto my bag, which was hanging off a branch in a tree, and the branch was breaking, and I jumped out to save her and then we fell, and then we were stuck in another tree, and you came along and saved us."

"Jackson, I never left this spot."

Jackson didn't know what to think. Meeka chewed on the ends of her hair. She was oddly quiet.

"Tell me the story again," Josh said. And Jackson told him. Josh nodded thoughtfully. "Jackson, I'm an apprentice. I don't have those kinds of powers, nor privileges. I'm only allowed to lead you to the river and tell you what to do. The rest was up to you. I've been sitting here, waiting for you and studying my apprentice's book."

"Then who was there? It looked like you, it sounded like you, it had to be you!"

Josh looked out over the river. "Jackson, I think you just met the Author."

A Chapter that Explains the Author ... Even More!

Jackson's insides churned. He was nervous, but a happy kind of nervous.

"How could I have met the Author? He looked like you."

Josh was thoughtful. "I don't know. But I think you did. It's very rare, but I have read of circumstances where the Author steps out and reveals himself to the one seeking."

"But I wasn't seeking him!" Jackson argued. "And besides, he didn't reveal himself! It was you!"

Josh frowned for a moment in concentration. "I think I read about this in Section 24A of my apprentice book." He rifled through its pages. "Okay, 'The Author will occasionally reveal himself when the occasion is appropriate. The Author may take any shape or form to best suit the interaction between himself and the Seeker,'" he quoted.

"But why did he look like you?"

Josh shook his head. "I don't know. Usually the Author takes the form of someone Seekers know well, or someone they trust. Do you trust me? Is that it?"

Jackson ruminated. (*Ruminated* is like when you think about something so hard you feel like your head is going to explode. Not really explode. Just feel like it.

Oh, never mind.) Then he looked up at Josh. "Yeah, for some strange reason, I trust you."

Josh nodded, smiling at Jackson. "So what made you choose those stones?" He took the stones from Jackson and examined them closely.

"I don't know. I picked up different stones that had writing on them, but ..."

"But?"

Jackson looked down at his feet. "Well, maybe they were true. But they said stuff like, *You have a bad haircut, You're bad at baseball, You are stupid, You have no friends* ..." Jackson's voice trailed off.

"What else did they say?" Josh prodded gently.

Jackson quickly rubbed his eyes. "*You are not ... worth loving. Your dreams are not real. You are not special.*" Jackson stopped. His throat had a large lump stuck in it.

Josh laid his hand gently on Jackson's shoulder. Jackson didn't look up at him.

"Jackson," he whispered.

Jackson found the ground moss fascinating.

"Jackson. Look at me."

Jackson wiped his eyes again and looked up at him. His eyes hurt, and his face felt hot.

"Jackson, do you really believe all those things?" Josh asked.

Jackson shrugged and looked over Josh's shoulder, not answering.

"Even after what you saw in the mirrors? Even after what you read in the Book?" Josh asked. Jackson sighed deeply. He was so confused. He wanted to believe those things, but ...

"I'm so confused. I want to believe those things ..." he trailed off.

Josh nodded. "Sometimes it's easier to believe the bad stuff, isn't it?"

Jackson sniffed loudly.

"Jackson, do you believe that the Author made you?" he asked.

Jackson nodded slowly.

"Do you believe that the Author loves you?"

Jackson's head was filled with muddled thoughts.

Do I believe the Author loves me?

I have no idea.

How could I even know that?

I mean, Eleissa and Meeka and Josh seem to think he loves them, but how would they know?

I can understand why he would love Eleissa because she's so smart. And Meeka is so funny and lovable. And Josh is really cool. Who wouldn't love him?

But what about me?

I'm not smart or funny or cool. But ...

If the Author made me, he knew I would mess up. So then why would he make me if he knew I was going to mess up all the time?

Why would he make me if he knew I wouldn't be cool and have friends?

Why would he make me if he knew that I would be terrible at baseball?

Why would he even let me want to play if I'm so awful?

Wait a minute.

Wait a minute!

What if . . .

. . . if he already knew, if he already knows everything about me, and yet, he made me anyway . . .

. . . why?

Mom and Dad love me even though I mess up. Dad tells me to keep practicing, and Mom hugs me even when I make her mad. They don't care that I'm not cool. They don't care that I suck at baseball. And they always read my stories. It's obvious they love me.

Maybe that's it.

It doesn't matter if I'm cool or good at baseball or smart . . .

Maybe the Author made me just because. . .

. . . because he loves me. How could someone make something and not love it?

"Yes. I do believe the Author loves me," Jackson said finally. "And I think it doesn't matter whether I'm smart or cool or . . ."

Josh nodded eagerly.

"He just . . . wants me to follow my dreams, to find the purpose he planned for me."

"So then why did you pick the white stones?" Josh asked.

"I chose the white stones because they were calling to me." Jackson felt a little silly saying that, but so many silly things had happened that night, this didn't seem too strange.

"Go on," Josh encouraged.

"I was lying down in the river and I heard my name. I couldn't figure out who or what was speaking, but when I picked up the white stones and listened, they were calling me. So these stones had to be mine, right? I mean, that seems a logical explanation to me."

Josh smiled. "Jackson, sometimes all you have to do is be quiet and listen. I know you're only ten and a half, but you're growing up. And there will be times in your life when you will have quiet in your life that is not self-created. And during those times you'll be struggling and searching, and bitterness and heart-ache will find you. That's when you'll discover the answers. Life is hard. Life is painful. But without hardships and pain, you'll never grow as a person. You'll never develop confidence or character or hope. But here's the cool part—in all of those struggles, during all those times you want to give up, you *need* to be quiet and you *need* to be still, because otherwise you won't hear the answers."

"What answers?" Jackson asked.

"Answers to what you have to do. Answers on where to go. Answers to who you are. To quote the Author, 'in quietness and in confidence shall be your strength.'"

Josh pointed at the river. "The test in the river was that you could have picked any of the white stones. You could have taken one step into the river and stepped right out again with one of them in your hand."

"Why didn't you tell me that? I almost *died* in the waterfall!"

"But you didn't die, did you?" Josh asked.

"That's what I said!" chirped Meeka. Josh looked over at her and smiled. She sat back down, pleased with herself.

"You didn't die. The Author was probably testing you," Josh said.

"Testing me for what? I nearly died!" Jackson repeated loudly.

"Jackson. From what you told me, Meeka was hang-ing on for her life to that satchel, right?"

Jackson nodded.

"You risked your own life to save hers, even though there was the chance that you would die."

"Well, it's not like I had much choice!"

"Actually, you did have a choice. You could have let her fall."

"I couldn't have let Meeka die!"

Josh nodded. "And that's what makes you who you are. You didn't worry about what could happen to you. You just had to save her, no matter what. And that is what faith is. You just stepped out to save her. You knew, way back in your mind, that somehow, if you could save her, the Author would make sure that everything would be okay. You didn't think of yourself. The Author tested your faith and found it abundant. You, Jackson, are a man of great loyalty, great courage, and great selflessness. And those are very admirable qualities indeed," Josh finished.

"But what about the stones?" Jackson asked.

"Jackson, it's easy to pick up any stone. It's easy to believe lies. There are lies all around us, and they are easy to see. But these white stones, they don't tell you who you are; they are just part of the journey to figuring it out. No one can tell you who you are, because deep down, you know who you are. You are who the Author created you to be. You are yourself. The white stones are everywhere, but it's easier to find the ones that lie. It's up to us to choose what to believe.

"Two voices are always speaking to us. One helps us be who we are; the other tells us how we fail. One wants to encourage us, to tell us that we are awesome and wonderful because the Author created us, and the other wants to tear us to shreds so that we become nothing. Just bits of nothingness, barely making it through life. You always have a choice in which voice to believe. And once you believe the true voice, you have to hang to what it says and not listen to the other voice," Josh explained.

Jackson was quiet. He thought about the stones etched with lies. As easy as it was to believe them, he liked the idea of believing the Author instead. "So I guess I have a lot to look forward to, growing up I mean. I didn't know it would be so hard."

"Of course life is hard. No one ever said it was easy. I mean, you still have high school and acne to deal with, college courses to pick, debts to pay, a career to decide, bills, taxes, politics, and telemarketers. It's all ugly and it's all annoying." Josh laughed. "It sure is fun though."

"How can you say its fun? It sounds awful! I don't want to grow up to that!"

Josh smiled. "It's fun because you find your fun. In high school you'll get smarter, you'll figure things out, and you'll make new friends. In college you'll get to study something you want to learn. You'll get a job that you like, or at least one that pays the bills and taxes so you can do what you love to do. Joy is where you look for it.

"Do you have the Book?" Josh asked.

Jackson handed it to him. "It got all wet. I think it's ruined."

Josh held it gently. He shook it gently and water droplets flew everywhere. He handed it back to Jackson.

"Open it," he said.

Jackson opened the Book to the first page. It opened easily. It was completely dry, and the pages were intact.

You are smart, it read. Jackson turned the page.

You are a good baseball player, read the next page. Jackson smiled and kept turning pages.

You are worthy, said the next.

You seek out the truth.

Jackson turned the next page.

You were created for a purpose.

Jackson looked up at Josh. "What purpose?"

"That, my friend, is a question that only you can answer—with some help from the One who created you. I bet you'll have an awesome time trying to find out."

Jackson smiled. He felt pretty good, actually.

"I bet you're pretty hungry and tired about now," Josh speculated.

Jackson nodded vigorously. He was so hungry, he could eat his arm.

Josh pointed at the river. "Go ahead and take a drink. It'll make you feel better."

Jackson shuddered. "Are you kidding? It's gross! I fell into it awhile ago, and I got some of it in my mouth and that was disgusting!"

Josh paused. "Was the water clean or dirty?"

"It was filthy! It was all sludge and muddy and slimy and gross."

Josh nodded. "You saw what you wanted to see. Your struggles and frustrations caused the scenery around you to change. If you had kept reminding yourself of who you were, remaining confident, you would have seen a very different river. Now, what you need to do is see the truth. The river is very clean and very filling. Go ahead and drink."

Jackson dragged his poor, tired body to the river. He looked into it and saw a sandy bottom with stones scattered all about. He looked closer and saw little bugs floating on the top. The fish were darting to and fro, stirring up the light sand from the bottom.

"But there's ... there's *fish* in here! And *bugs!* And I don't even want to *know* what that floating stuff is!"

"Close your eyes and drink!" Josh laughed.

Jackson stifled a groan. He squatted down and scooped up the cool water in his hands. He caught a bug and a twig. He shut his eyes tightly and brought his hands to his lips. He could feel the bug tickling his lips. He tried not to gag.

He swallowed.

In Which Jackson May Drink Bugs

The water slipped into Jackson's mouth. His lips were numbed by the cold, and he couldn't feel his tongue. He wanted to spit it out but he swallowed instead. He felt the water slip down his throat and into his stomach. The numbing continued past his stomach and into his legs, then to his feet. It rushed into his arms and fingertips, then into his head and right to the very ends of his messy hair. And all at once the tingling stopped. Jackson opened his eyes, and then he stared in amazement.

The river changed. It had turned a bright, vibrant blue. The river's bottom was laid with gold bricks. Orange and purple violets covered the riverbank, their heads turned to the sun. And then Jackson looked up into the sky and saw a rainbow. Not a rainbow *in* the sky, you see, for the sky itself was a rainbow. Long stripes of reds, blues, purples, yellows, oranges, and greens, all of them filling the sky. Jackson's heart swelled. He splashed into the river and dunked his head into the water. He laughed and drank deeply. It was the best water he ever tasted. He sat up and looked back at Josh.

Josh's body glowed. His uniform was a bright glow-ing white, with not a smudge of dirt on it. A golden-yellow light encircled him.

Jackson was at a loss for words. "Josh?" he asked.

Josh smiled.

"Uh, can I take some of this water home?" Jackson asked.

Josh laughed. "No. And it's time to go."

Jackson looked down into the river, but it had changed back again. The water was just a regular river color, the trees were golden weeping willows, and the banks were just grass again.

Jackson climbed out of the river and walked over to Josh, who was no longer wearing white. "What was that? Why did it change? What did you change? What's going on?"

Josh smiled broadly at Jackson. "What you saw was a present for you, from the Author. Hold on to that memory."

Josh dug into the pocket of his satchel and pulled something out. He placed it into Jackson's hand.

It was a key. A plain, old-fashioned, gold (but slightly tarnished) key.

"Give it to Great-Aunt Harriett when the time is right," Josh said.

"What do you mean? When will I know?"

Josh smiled mysteriously. "You'll know." He picked up the Book and handed it to Jackson.

"Now hang on to this Book. It holds the truth about your life." Josh handed him two of the white stones. "And hold on to these, because they'll remind you to believe in the truth." He hugged Jackson fiercely. "Give Harriett a hug for me."

"You know my Great-Aunt Harriett?"

Josh looked at the river and smiled, lost in thought. He nodded his head slowly and turned to Jackson. "Don't ever give up, my friend. You have what it takes," Josh said. He began to walk away.

"Wait a minute! Will I ever see you again? I mean, can we hang out sometime?" yelled Jackson.

"When it's time!" Josh called.

"But how do you know my Great-Aunt Harriett? I mean, how does she know you?" Jackson called.

"She's my mom!"

And then he was gone.

In Which They Rush Home

"So what's next on the Tour, Meeka?" Jackson asked. Meeka shook her head sadly. "I'm afraid the Tour is over."

Jackson stopped. "What do you mean?"

"Jackson, as much fun as it was, as much as I like you, you have to go back. You've been here all night. And I have to give other tours. It *is* part of my *job* you know."

Jackson looked at his watch. Six thirty! His mom would be downstairs making breakfast and coming to wake him up in half an hour!

"Meeka, I have to get back by seven!" he yelled.

"Okay, but hang on!" Meeka jumped into the river, making a big splash. She dug furiously in her work satchel and pulled out the slimy, dead fish. She bent down and carefully held him in the water. His still body shuddered, his tail flicked, and he swam away.

"What the . . . ? Meeka! Why did you have that dead fish in your bag?" Jackson asked.

"No time, no time! Follow me!" she yelled. And she took off.

Meeka and Jackson ran down the halls, turned corners, climbed up stairs, climbed down stairs, and felt their way through a dark room ("It's a shortcut!") until they found themselves breathing heavily beside a door.

Meeka threw her arms around Jackson, hugging him so tightly, he couldn't breathe. And on top of not being able to breathe because he was out of breath, that's a lot of not breathing.

He hugged her back.

"I'm going to miss you, Jackson." A few tears fell down her little elf face.

"I'm going to miss you too, Meeka. It's great finally having a friend."

"Best friend?" she asked.

"Yeah, best friend," he agreed.

Meeka smiled a wobbly smile and said, "I'll need your glasses."

"Can I visit again?" he asked.

"Only if you find us."

"How am I supposed to find you? Do I just climb into Great-Aunt Harriett's hair again?" But Meeka had slipped the glasses off Jackson's head, and he saw nothing but hair. "Meeka? How am I supposed to find you?" he called out. But a big wad of hair went in his mouth, and he started to choke. Jackson felt little hands on his back, and he was shoved hard.

chapter 67

In Which Jackson
Hits the Floor

Jackson hit the floor with a thud.

"Landth thaketh alive, child! Can't you aim bettaw when you faww out of bed? You almotht few on me!" Actually what she *said* was, "Land's sakes alive, child! Can't you aim better when you fall out of bed! You almost fell on me!" but I've translated for you. Again.

Jackson opened his eyes. He was in his room, on the floor. Great-Aunt Harriett stood over him, her eyes peering at him quite intently.

"Who's Josh?" he blurted.

Her eyes cleared for a moment. "Josh," she whispered. The look was gone, and her eyes clouded over again. "Well, let's go downstairs," she said. "I need some medicine for my awful headache. What dreams I had!" she said. She trudged toward the door and she paused. "Josh," she whispered. "Such dreams I had."

She shook her head and scuffled down the hall.

chapter

68

A Chapter that Has a Key, a Book, and a Picture

Jackson! Breakfast! Hurry up and get dressed!" his mom called from downstairs.

Jackson saw the satchel beside him on the floor. It was worn and dirty and the strap was ripped. It couldn't have been a dream, could it?

Jackson quickly shoved his hands in his pockets, searching.

He pulled out a key.

A plain, old-fashioned, gold key.

He grabbed his satchel and ripped it open, trembling with anticipation. He pulled out the Book and two white stones. He opened the Book's pages and a picture slipped onto the floor. Jackson picked it up. It was a picture of a house. The house where he met Rayaa and Eleissa. In the picture, the front door was covered with huge, wispy cobwebs attached in six different spots with gargantuan, hairy-backed spiders waiting for their lunch. The house had big boards nailed across it. And a skull-and-crossbones sign beside it. There was even a big hole in the porch floor.

"Jackson! Let's go!" his mom yelled.

Jackson tucked the Book into the makeshift tent on his bunk. He changed out of his pajamas into jeans and a T-shirt. He pocketed the key and the two stones. He tossed his sneakers into his closet.

And he went downstairs.

In Which Jackson Has an Idea

"Where did you get that?" his mom asked.

Jackson was eating whole-wheat blueberry pancakes with dark maple syrup. The picture was propped up on the table beside him.

"Oh ... um ... nowhere. It's just a picture of a house," he said.

"Hm ... It looks really familiar. I'm sure I've seen that house before," she thought aloud.

The house did look familiar. Jackson couldn't shake the feeling that he had also seen it before, somewhere else.

After breakfast, everyone agreed they would go out shopping. Jackson asked if he could stay home. His mom looked at him with a raised eyebrow and then said, "We're only ten minutes away, so if there are any problems, call me. And Mrs. Smith is home next door if you're desperate."

Jackson barely heard her, because he had just had an idea.

He waited until his family climbed into the car and drove down the street. He went into the living room and sat down on the floor in front of the wall unit. He opened the cupboard door and pulled out all of the photo albums. He flipped page after page, looking at old photos. He had definitely seen that house before. Somewhere.

Two hours passed and Jackson was fed up. But in a nice way. Like when you're just tired of looking. Not the kind where you start throwing things because you're frustrated. (Which by the way, is a rude way of behaving, and there is absolutely no reason for behavior like that. Just ask your mom.)

Jackson pulled out the last photo album.

Of course the photo was in there. How could it not be? It was the last photo album. Things are never in the first place you look, always the last. If only there was a way to look at the last place you would look first, and not the other way around, then you would save a lot of time in finding things.

Jackson saw it.

The House.

Jackson held up his photo beside it. It looked the same. Except that the front door in this picture was a perfectly good way to go in. It didn't have huge,

wispy cobwebs attached in six different spots with gargantuan, hairy-backed spiders waiting for their lunch. And the door didn't have big boards nailed across it with a skull-and-crossbones sign beside it. The big hole in the porch floor didn't exist. *This* house was quite lovely. And there was Great-Aunt Harriett, standing on the pathway. She was smiling. Her hair was surprisingly short. And beside her on the grass was a little bassinet. Jackson took the photo out of its sleeve and turned it over. *Harriett and Josh, summer of 1960.* Jackson's jaw dropped. Was Josh ... was Josh really Great-Aunt Harriett's son? What was he doing in her hair? Jackson was very confused.

At that moment, everyone came home. It was chaos. The dog barked, Jackson's little sister was crying, his dad tripped over the barking dog and spilled the bags of groceries, and his brother ran to the washroom ... chaos. Jackson's mom came into the living room where Jackson was sitting.

"Anything happen while we were gone? Did the mail come?" she stopped and looked at him curiously. "What are you doing?"

"Mom, did Great-Aunt Harriett grow up in this house?" he asked, showing her the photograph.

She took the photo from him and studied it quietly. She smiled wistfully. "I had forgotten about that house. It was a great house. I used to spend my summers there when I was a little girl. Aunt Harriett had the most beautiful gardens and so many birds. I used to think she had every bird in the world in her backyard. And she had that crazy cedar maze. I used to love playing there. Josh and I ..." she trailed off.

"Who's Josh?"

She cleared her throat. "Josh was Aunt Harriett's son. He died very young. Awful car accident. It broke Aunt Harriett's heart. She was never really the same after that."

"Do you think the house is still there?" he asked.

"I doubt it, honey. It's been so long. It was probably sold and the property turned into a mall or a car lot or something." She gave the photo back to Jackson.

"Can we go look?"

"Oh, buddy, it's pretty far. I don't think it's there anymore." And then she looked at Jackson.

Sometimes, just sometimes, your mom gets it. She just has to look in your eyes, and she knows how important something is to you. She knows that it is something you just *have* to do. And at that moment, Jackson's mom got it.

She smiled at him. "I'll get the car keys."

"Can Great-Aunt Harriett come?"

She paused. "I don't know if that's a good idea. It might hurt her heart to see her house gone. And it might bring back some unhappy memories about Josh."

"Please?"

"Okay, go get her. I'll start the car."

A Chapter that Involves the High Price of Lattes

Jackson ran up the stairs and found Great-Aunt Harriett packing her bag.

"Great-Aunt Harriett, would you like to go for a drive?" he asked.

"Yes, (I translated again for you so we can finish this story and get on with our school day, work day, life in general . . .) yes, I do hear the birds! They are so lovely this time of year," she said. She stood up and looked out the window. The soft breeze blew, but nary a hair on her head moved.

Jackson took her hand and carefully led her downstairs. "Yes, Great-Aunt Harriett, the birds are lovely this time of year. Why don't we go for a drive and look for them?"

"Coffee? I don't want to go for coffee! Land's sakes, child, it'll me keep me awake until next week! And the prices for a chai latte! Ridiculous, if you ask me!"

chapter 71

A Chapter that Involves Anticipation, a Car Ride, and Cow Poop

The car ride was very long. Jackson sat in the back seat, alternatively looking outside and at the two photos he held in his hands. The rows of houses gave way to trees, and the trees gave way to open fields. Farmhouses with red roofs and red barns with tall silos could be seen in the distance. The smell of cow poop hung in the air. The pavement soon turned to tar-and-chip roads and then to dusty gravel. During all this time, Jackson entertained many, many thoughts. Such as:

I wonder if the house is still there. I wonder if it has changed much. I wonder if I can visit Meeka again. How on earth am I going to climb back into Great-Aunt Harriett's hair? I wonder if she'd notice. Gosh, I am so tired! I can't let my mom know that I'm tired because then she won't let me read in bed anymore! I don't know if she'd even believe me if I told her where I've been! Or maybe she would. Huh. I wonder if the house will be the same on the inside. I wonder if Eleissa will be in one of the rooms, reading her big book. I wonder if Rayaa will be outside hunting crubbies? Do crubbies actually exist? Did I just dream all of this? How could it be a dream if

I've got a key and two white stones in my pocket? I wonder if I can see Meeka again. Why did I see Josh if he
died so many years ago? Am I losing my mind? What if I
turn out like Great-Aunt Harriett and don't know a tuba
from a bassoon? What is the cosine of 7.88? And how do
you say 'couch' in Spanish?

And so on.

But the one thought that returned, the one thought
that made him hold his breath the whole way there,
figuratively speaking, of course, was, *I hope the house
is still there.* Jackson was on the edge of his seat with
excitement, fear, and expectancy. *It just has to be there.
It just has to ...*

They turned a corner.

A Chapter that Has More Words in the Title than in the Chapter

There it was.

In Which a House Is Found

The house was faded red brick with a wraparound porch covered with peeling white paint. There were weeds blocking the path from the road to the door. The roof's black shingles were curling back with age. The trees out front were overgrown and ugly. The house was old and tired.

It was beautiful.

Jackson jumped out of the car and ran up the weedy path.

"Jackson! Be careful!" his mom cried out.

Jackson leapt up the front steps, avoiding the large hole in front of the door. He brushed off the wispy spiderwebs and flipped away gargantuan spiders with hairy backs. He feverishly pulled at the boards nailed over the door, and they came away in his hands. He turned the doorknob and ...

He stood in the hall. A long hall with faded ultramarine blue walls. Little red tables covered with thick dust lined the hallway. Above the little red tables, faded mirrors hung on the walls.

Jackson smiled. He took a deep breath and coughed. The place was filthy.

"I don't believe it." Jackson's mom stood beside him in the hallway. "I haven't been here in a really long time," she said looking around. She took a few steps

253

toward a mirror and, raising her hand, swept away the grime. She looked into the mirror intently, very quiet. She didn't move.

"M-mom?" Jackson asked hesitantly.

Her eyes turned to him and she looked surprised to see him. She looked back at the mirror. "Huh."

"What do you see?" Jackson whispered as he took her hand.

His mom smiled and shrugged her shoulders. "Just remembering, stuff." She laughed out loud, running her hand through her hair. "I'm getting old."

Jackson hugged her. "You're not old to me." She hugged him back tightly.

"I *am* getting old ..." she looked back into the mirror. "Find your story," she whispered softly. She turned back to Jackson. "I'd better go get Aunt Harriett. She might have fallen down a hole or something." She winked at him and went outside.

Jackson looked into the mirror. Looking back at him was a rather plain-looking boy ten-and-a-half-years old, one who was no longer friendless. Jackson put his hand in his pocket, squeezed the two white stones, and smiled.

He walked down the hall toward where Eleissa's room should have been. He saw the blue wall and walked toward the door. He took the handle and turned it, holding his breath, hoping.

The room was filled with books sitting neatly on their bookshelves. The windows were dusty. He could almost see Eleissa's tent filled with pillows. He could see her reading her book and then looking up at him with her wise blue eyes.

"Jackson! Come on outside!" his mom called. Jackson smiled at the room. Then he went outside.

He followed the porch around the side of the house and saw the cedar maze. It was tall and overgrown. The tops were uneven. Great-Aunt Harriett stood at the gate, her old gnarled hands holding the rails.

Jackson walked to Great-Aunt Harriett, staring at her. She looked different. She seemed ... taller. Was that possible? Her hair was, well, shorter. If that's even possible.

Her eyes shone. "I remember ... can you hear the birds? Jackson! I have to see the birds!" She grabbed his hand and squeezed it urgently. Jackson dug into his pocket and held out the gold key. She looked down at it and began to laugh then took it carefully from his hand and put it into the lock. The gate swung open. She stepped down the back porch steps and turned right toward the maze. Jackson and his mom followed.

Great-Aunt Harriett walked faster and faster. She walked with determination and purpose. Jackson had to run a little to keep up. He didn't want to lose her in the maze.

Great-Aunt Harriett laughed. "They might still be there!" she cried out, and started to run. Jackson followed her with his mom following behind.

They turned a corner and ...

There it was.

In Which Birds Are Very Loud

The birdcage.

The big, beautiful, golden birdcage.

But it was dirty.

And rusted.

And empty.

Great-Aunt Harriett ran up to the cage, and her old fingers clasped the bars. She closed her eyes and smiled. "Listen," she said. "You can hear them singing."

Jackson looked into the sky and the trees, but he didn't see any birds. Great-Aunt Harriett's eyes were squeezed shut as she listened intently. Jackson closed his eyes, straining to hear. It was very faint at first, but the sound grew louder. The singing penetrated his heart. He opened his eyes and gasped.

There, inside the open birdcage, were many, many birds. Not the birds he had seen on his adventure, but birds nonetheless. They were singing, their voices in harmony with each other. Great-Aunt Harriett laughed. She laughed so hard that she lay down on the ground. Jackson and his mom lay down beside Great-Aunt Harriett. The three of them looked up into the sky.

"Just seeing this house brings back a lot of memories," his mom murmured. Jackson turned his head to look at Great-Aunt Harriett.

She looked so different—beautiful almost. Her hair no longer resembled a wedding cake. It spread loosely around her like a halo. Her eyes were closed, and she was smiling. She looked peaceful. She opened her eyes and looked at Jackson.

"I wonder if it's still there," she whispered.

"If what's still there?" asked Jackson.

But Great-Aunt Harriett didn't answer. She sat up and pulled herself effortlessly to her feet. She walked back into the cedar maze and chose an opening.

Jackson got up and followed her. Her fingers trailed along the cedar walls, as she hummed to herself. Jackson kept following.

Great-Aunt Harriett turned left and there . . .

. . . was a potting shed.

In Which Jackson Finds Another Door

Gray moss grew on the faded black roof. The windows were covered with dirt and the garden boxes were full of weeds. The door was a chipped blue, tucked into weathered cedar planks. Great-Aunt Harriett trembled beside Jackson. She handed him the key.

"Will ... will you unlock the door, Jackson?" she asked, her voice high and excited and terrified all at once.

Jackson took the key from her trembling fingers and slid it into the lock. It stuck for a moment but then turned. The door swung open. It was very dark inside. And musty. And dirty. Jackson sneezed.

Great-Aunt Harriett stepped inside. She stood for a moment, looking at her surroundings, then quickly strode to the windows. She yanked open the shutters and a bit of light came through. Jackson saw a little potting table and chair in the corner. The top of the table was dirty, and the soil smelled musty and dank. Empty pots lay on their sides, and stacked piles of pots waited to be filled.

Great-Aunt Harriett knelt down in the dust and swept away the dirt with her gnarled hands.

"Help me," she cried urgently.

Jackson knelt down beside her and swept the dirt away with his palms.

And found a door in the floor!

Jackson grabbed the handle and pulled. Locked.

Great-Aunt Harriett reached around to the back of her neck and undid a necklace. A charm hung on it. A small key. She put the key into the lock and turned it. Jackson lifted the handle and the door opened.

A Chapter that Involves
Another Place

Jackson peeked into the hole below but saw nothing. "What's down there?"

Great-Aunt Harriett smiled, tears running down her face. "Another place," she said. Jackson looked at her in amazement. She wasn't lisping anymore! How? What? Why? Huh.

She maneuvered her body to sit on the edge, her legs dangling into the dark hole. Jackson was a little worried. "Should you be climbing down there? I don't see any stairs. You could hurt yourself," he said.

Great-Aunt Harriett placed her hand on Jackson's cheek. Her clear eyes were bright blue.

"Jackson, you've given me a great gift. I forgot this place existed. I used to come here as a little girl. It's a ... it's a door to another place. A place I loved to visit. A place where rooms have rivers, where bookstores sell magical books, and where elves live. Where Josh went when ..." she cleared her throat and wiped her eyes.

"I used to come here all the time as a child. I even used to bring your mom here, although I doubt she remembers. Such an amazing place that the Author made," she said.

Jackson was speechless.

She hugged him tightly. "Thank you. Come visit soon. You'll love Meeka." Then she pinched his cheek. Not too hard though. "Go find your story, Jackson!"

She jumped.

chapter 77

In Which We Learn More

Jackson cried out. He waited for her to hit the bottom or yell or something. There wasn't any noise.

"Great-Aunt Harriett! Are you okay?" he yelled. But there was no answer. Just quiet. Jackson felt a calming peace fill him. Something told him that she was okay. That maybe, just maybe, this was a door to where he had been. But how did that make sense?

Jackson stepped out of the shed and saw his mom. She walked slowly toward him with a very serious, grown-up look on her face.

"Did she jump?" she asked.

Jackson was surprised, but he nodded.

"She probably won't come back," she said.

Jackson nodded again. "She told me that you used to go there."

"When I was younger," she paused. "I thought places like this didn't last."

She smiled.

In Which We Learn
Even More

Jackson and his mom walked back to the house holding hands. They hadn't held hands in a long time, and she missed that. Any mother reading this will know the feeling.

They climbed up the back steps and opened the welcoming back door. Dust danced in the sunlight that seeped through the windows. The large crystal chandelier cast one or two feeble rainbows on the walls. The hallway of tables and mirrors mounted in old gilt frames beckoned them in.

"Mom?"

"Yeah?"

"Great-Aunt Harriett changed. I mean, well, her hair got uh, smaller. And she grew. Like she got taller. And she wasn't lisping anymore!" Jackson blurted.

Her eyebrows frowned thoughtfully. "Well," she began slowly. "I guess it was time for her to be her real self."

"What does that mean? Be her real self?" Jackson asked. He didn't understand at all. "I don't understand at all."

"I think when you get older, you'll understand better."

"What? That's not fair! Tell me now!"

Jackson's mom smiled at him. "Have you ever heard of the Author?"

They were interrupted by a tinkling in the air, of something magical happening.

A pink envelope appeared on a red table.

Jackson picked it up and turned it over in his hands. He handed it to his mom and she opened it.

She read it out loud.

This is what it said, exactly.

Welcome Home!
Enclosed is the deed to the house.
Take care of it,
It's yours!

The Author

Jackson hugged his mom. She held him tightly.

"We should go visit them soon," she said.

Jackson agreed, hugging her tighter.

chapter

Epilogue

A couple of questions weren't answered for you, so I'm answering them for you now.

The cosine of 7.88 is 0.99055738.

The Spanish word for "couch" is *el sofa*.

And I suppose you have more questions.

Will there be another book? Will there be a prequel so you can read more about Meeka and Rayaa and Eleissa? Will you find out if Rayaa and Eleissa were promoted? Does Meeka ever get promoted? Does Great-Aunt Harriett find Josh? Does Jackson ever return to where they all are? How does he get there? What is that place anyway? Can I go there?

The answers to these questions are: Probably. I think so. I don't see why not. I think she could be, but it'll take awhile. Probably. I don't see why not. I can't say. You'll get it someday. Only if you get it.

The End

chapter

Acknowledgements

First and foremost, thank you, Lord, for making this dream come true!

Thank you, Danny, for working two jobs. Thank you for never complaining about my lack of housekeeping skills. You see me and you know my heart. I love you, and you are my hero. Here's to Paris.

Thank you to all of my encouraging fans, especially the ones who were there from the beginning. Thank you to my three Glennie girls for letting me borrow your wonderful personalities and idiosyncrasies. Thank you to Burb, who effortlessly edited what she could, and to Zuzu for letting me borrow Josh. Thank you, Suzanne. Thank you to Gigi, who told me I *had* to write another one. Thank you to Sylvia, who gave me *The Dreamgiver* and told me to just write it. Thank you to Andy Meisenheimer, who saw potential in this crazy girl and put the manuscript right into the best hands. Thank you to Kathleen, my beautiful, genius editor who is brilliant at her job and is a brilliant friend. I can't wait to work with you more. And I can't wait for California. Disco balls and lattes, baby.

And finally, thank you to Jackson for being my hero. You are my heart walking around outside my body. Keep God in your heart and you'll never fail. Find your story, my little gaffer. I know it'll be awesome. I love you.

We want to hear from you. Please send your comments
about this book to us in care of zreview@zondervan.com. Thank you.

ZONDERVAN.com/
AUTHORTRACKER
follow your favorite authors